A VISUAL HISTORY OF COSTUME
The Twentieth Century

PENELOPE BYRDE

B. T. BATSFORD LTD · LONDON
DRAMA BOOK PUBLISHERS · NEW YORK

Acknowledgements

I should like to thank all the museums, art galleries, other institutions and collectors mentioned in the List of Illustrations for their kind co-operation and for supplying the photographs for this book. I am also very grateful to all those artists who have generously allowed me to reproduce their works of art in this volume. The names of individuals are too numerous to list again here but I hope they will take my thanks as read.

My thanks are due to Dr Aileen Ribeiro of the Courtauld Institute of Art and to Timothy Auger and Clare Sunderland of Batsford for making this book possible.

© Penelope Byrde 1986
First published 1986
Reprinted 1987

Reprinted in paperback 1992

ISBN 0 7134 6830 0

Typeset by Keyspools Ltd, Golborne, Lancs
and printed in Great Britain by
Courier International Ltd., East Kilbride

for the publishers
B. T. Batsford Ltd
4 Fitzhardinge Street
London W1H 0AH

Preface

A Visual History of Costume is a series devised for those who need reliable, easy-to-use reference material on the history of dress.

The central part of each book is a series of illustrations, in black-and-white and colour, taken from the time of the dress itself. They include oil paintings, photographs, illustrations and line drawings. By the use of such material, the reader is given a clear idea of what was worn and how, without the distortions and loss of detail which modern drawings can occasionally entail.

Each picture is captioned in a consistent way, under the headings, where appropriate, 'Head', 'Body' and 'Accessories'; the clothes are not just described, but their significance explained. The reader will want to know whether a certain style was fashionable or unfashionable at a certain time, usual or unusual — such information is clearly and consistently laid out. The illustrations are arranged in date order, and the colour illustrations are numbered in sequence with the black-and-white, so that the processes of change can be clearly followed.

The pictures will be all the better appreciated if the reader has at least some basic overall impression of the broad developments in dress in the period concerned, and the Introduction is intended to provide this.

Technical terms have been kept to a reasonable minimum. Many readers will use these books for reference, rather than read them straight through from beginning to end. To explain every term every time it is used would have been hopelessly repetitive, and so a Glossary has been provided. Since the basic items of dress recur throughout the book, a conventional, full Index would have been equally repetitive; therefore the Glossary has been designed also to act as an Index; after each entry the reader will find the numbers of those illustrations which show important examples of the item concerned.

Contents

List of Illustrations

Note The subject is followed by the artist, where known, then the medium, and then the collection. An asterisk * indicates a colour illustration, to be found between pages 120 and 121.

5

6

100　The Teaching Staff of the
Painting School, Royal College
of Art, 1949–50
Rodrigo Moynihan
Oil on canvas
Tate Gallery, London

101　Woman's suit by Worth
Anon. pen and watercolour on
paper, 1949–50
Fashion Research Centre, Bath

102　Accessories for Ascot
Anon. illustration from Harvey
Nichols store catalogue, 1950
Fashion Research Centre, Bath

103　*Conversation Piece at the Royal
Lodge, Windsor
James Gunn, 1950　Oil on canvas
National Portrait Gallery, London

104　Family Group (Lady Harlech,
Lord Salisbury, the Duchess of
Devonshire and Lord David
Cecil)
E. Halliday, 1951　Oil on canvas
Hatfield House, reproduced by
courtesy of the Marquess of
Salisbury
Photograph, Courtauld Institute of
Art, London

105　Advertisement for children's
clothes by Cherub
Charles Wood
Colour illustration from *Housewife*
magazine, 1952
Fashion Research Centre, Bath

106　Caroline
Robin Jacques
Line illustration to a short story in
Housewife magazine, 1953
Fashion Research Centre, Bath

107　Silks in May
Anon. colour illustration in Marshall
& Snelgrove store catalogue, 1954
Fashion Research Centre, Bath

108　From Narrow to Wide: Dior's 'A'
line
Anon. colour illustration from
Woman's Journal, 1955
Fashion Research Centre, Bath

109　Night into Day
Hof
advertisement by Simpsons in *The
Sketch*, 1955
Fashion Research Centre, Bath

110　Lady Pamela Berry
Anon. original photograph, 1956
Fashion Research Centre, Bath

111　The Pink Hat
Velma Ilsley
Illustration from *The Pink Hat*
published by J. B. Lippincott Co.,
Philadelphia and New York, 1956
Private collection

112　Casual clothes by Jaeger
Rene Gruau, 1956
Photograph, B. T. Batsford Ltd

113　Hugh Gaitskell
Judy Cassab, 1957
Oil on canvas
National Portrait Gallery, London

114　Teddy Boy wedding at
Lancaster
Anon. photograph, 1957
Syndication International

115　Saturday Night
Edward d'Arcy Lister, 1958
Oil on hardboard
Southampton Art Gallery

116　Dress and jacket by Harry B.
Popper
Alec Murray
Photograph for *The Sunday Times,*
1958
Fashion Research Centre, Bath

117　A Scene in Southam Street,
North Kensington
Christopher Hall, 1959
Oil on fibreboard
Museum of London

118　Skirts and jumpers
Anon. photograph for *The Sunday
Times*, 1959
Fashion Research Centre, Bath

119　Concert at the Chelsea Arts Club
Paul Wyeth, exhibited at the Royal
Academy, 1960
Oil on canvas
Chelsea Arts Club
Photograph, the Royal Academy of
Arts, London

120　Mrs David Muirhead
William Dring, R.A. 1960
Oil on canvas　Private collection
Photograph, the Royal Academy of
Arts, London

121　Helen Shapiro
Photograph, 1961

122　Evening dress by Victor Stiebel
Peter Clark　Photograph, 1962

123　Dress and hat by Mary Quant
John French
Photograph for *The Sunday Times*, 1963
Fashion Research Centre, Bath

124　The Beatles
Photograph, *c.* 1964

125　Executive Type
Peter Blake, 1964
Pencil on paper
Bristol City Art Gallery

126　Trouser suit by André Courrèges
Anon. pen and ink on paper, *The
Sunday Times*, 1964
Fashion Research Centre, Bath

127　Dinner suit by Harrods
Anon. illustration from Harrods
store catalogue, 1964
Fashion Research Centre, Bath

128　Dress by John Bates
John Bates, 1965
Ink on paper
Museum of Costume, Bath

129　Suit by Mary Quant
Anon. photograph for *The Sunday
Times*, 1966
Fashion Research Centre, Bath

130　Sir Francis Dashwood with his
wife and children
Claude Harrison, 1966
Oil on canvas
Sir Francis Dashwood Bt., West
Wycombe Park
Photograph, Courtauld Institute of
Art, London

131　Dress and PVC coat by Young
Jaeger
Norman Eales
Photograph for *The Sunday Times*, 1966
Fashion Research Centre, Bath

132　Julie Christie
Gerard de Rose, R.A. 1967
Oil on canvas
Photograph, Royal Academy of
Arts, London

133　The Bee Gees
Polydor publicity photograph, 1967

134　Mini-skirts and tops by Gina
Fratini
Christian Benais
Ink on paper, *The Sunday Times*.
1968
Fashion Research Centre, Bath

Introduction

The twentieth century, in its first three-quarters, has undoubtedly been a period of great change, in fashion as in every other field. Many of the developments associated with twentieth-century dress, however, had their roots in the second half of the nineteenth century. The sewing machine, chemical dyes, paper patterns and the first man-made fibre had all been invented before 1900, although it was some time before their potential was to be fully realized. Similarly, it was not until after 1900 that the long-term results of the fight for female emancipation, the development of shops and department stores, the emergence of the couturier or dress designer as an artist in his or her own right, and the nineteenth-century invention of photography were to have a fundamental effect on the course of fashion.

Where clothes are concerned, the present century differs from earlier periods in several respects – firstly, in the design and production of garments. At the beginning of the century it was still more usual for clothes to be individually made although a range of ready-to-wear garments was available. The most affluent and fashionable had their clothes made to measure, by a tailor (for men's clothes) and a couture house or Court dressmaker (for women's). Middle-class ladies could have a similar but less exclusive and expensive service at the larger shops and department stores (which ran their own dressmaking departments) or by going to an individual dressmaker; and many women made their own clothes at home. Britain looked to France for the lead in fashion and in Paris the haute couture houses set the style. Following the example of Charles Frederick Worth and Madame Paquin in the later nineteenth century, a number of new couture houses were established in the early 1900s, each with a talented dressmaker or designer at its head and known by name. The couturier became an important figure, regarded more as an artist than a tradesman. The originality and flair of designers such as Paul Poiret, Gabrielle Chanel, Madeleine Vionnet and Elsa Schiaparelli confirmed the pre-eminence of Paris as the centre of high fashion until the outbreak of the Second World War. After the War its reputation was again consolidated by the work of Christian Dior and Balenciaga, but since the 1950s, in spite of the talents of André Courrèges and Yves Saint Laurent, amongst others, the roles of Paris and of the exclusive, dictatorial haute couturier have been challenged and undermined. Fashion has become more international with designers in London, New York, Italy and Japan being recognized on an equal footing with those in Paris.

Furthermore, those in the ready-to-wear market are now as influential, if not more so, than those in traditional haute couture. Since the end of the Second World War there has also been the phenomenon of fashion emerging from the lower strata of society – young people, and often working-class groups, evolving original styles of dress which owe little or nothing to the fashion 'establishment' but which have made a vital contribution to it in terms of ideas and direction. Obvious examples are the Teddy Boys and Pop culture of the 1950s and 1960s, the Mods and Rockers, Hippies, Skinheads and in the 1970s, the Punks.

The increasing importance of ready-made clothing has been one of the most striking features in the history of twentieth-century costume and this had led to a new standardization of fashionable dress. The mass-production of clothes followed the invention of the sewing machine, in the mid-nineteenth century, surprisingly slowly; and during the first half of the twentieth century off-the-peg garments (especially in the case of men's clothes) tended to be regarded as inferior to those made to measure. However, technical advances and improvements in sizing resulted in the eventual manufacture of well-made and well-fitting garments at reasonable prices and these have been worn by the majority of people since the end of the Second World War.

Another notable feature of twentieth-century dress is the development of man-made fibres which has contributed to the production of practical, inexpensive clothing. The first man-made fibre imitated silk and was known as rayon after 1924; nylon appeared in America in 1938. These were followed by a number of other synthetic fibres, acrylics, viscoses and polyesters, called by various names. These have been used on their own to produce completely new fabrics or blended with natural fibres (which are now relatively expensive). Apart from the man-made fibres, two other materials have played an important role in twentieth-century dress design although they were created much earlier. One is hand- or machine-knitted fabric which has been used much more extensively than in other periods and the other is denim, for jeans, a revival of nineteenth-century American workmen's overalls. Modern clothes also incorporate new types of fastenings such as the press stud and the zip (invented at the beginning of the century) apart from a widespread use of elastic which first appeared in the nineteenth century.

The ways in which clothes are bought and sold have become highly organized and profitable industries. The Edwardian period saw the expansion of the department store and the establishment of new clothes shops. Later there followed the multiple or chain stores and from the late 1950s the boutiques: small specialist shops often providing a sympathetic ambience to customers. Good shopping facilities have become accessible to almost everyone and the same range of goods available almost simultaneously in London and the provinces. This and the methods of marketing and promoting fashion have ensured that news of changing styles is rapidly transmitted. The fashion show, the professional fashion model and even the mannequins in shop windows are twentieth-century developments which have made it possible to package and present new ideas and images very efficiently to a wide-ranging audience. The tradition since the late eighteenth century of carrying fashion news in newspapers and magazines has continued but engraved plates have been largely superseded by photographs. Advertising has become a sophisticated technique, extending to television and radio as well as the printed media.

Attitudes to clothes and the way they are worn have differed from earlier centuries in several ways. Since 1900 there has been a steady diminution in the amount of clothing worn by men, women and children. This has been perhaps more noticeable in the case of women who have adopted the short skirt and abandoned tightly-laced corsets in favour of increasingly lighter and briefer undergarments; but men have generally accepted lighter-weight cloths for suits and since the 1950s have regarded the waistcoat as an optional extra rather than an essential component of the suit. The adoption of lighter clothing both indoors and out has been to a great extent the result of improved heating and ventilation in houses, offices, private and public transport – people who travel habitually by car, for instance, rarely need to wear a heavy overcoat. This trend may also be attributable, less directly, to a gradual decrease in formality in dress. Compared with the generally rigid etiquette of the Victorian and Edwardian periods, dress in the later twentieth century has appeared to follow easier and less exacting rules: hats and gloves are no longer obligatory for most occasions, evening dress has become much less formal and sportswear more popular. Nevertheless rules of dress remain and a degree of formality is still observed in the clothes worn in offices and by the professions; if mourning has largely disappeared, weddings are, if anything, more elaborate.

While the form and shape of men's clothes have not altered fundamentally since 1900, women's clothes have become indisputably less restricting and more rational or functional during this period, reflecting the more fundamental change in the female role. Apart from the rejection of tight-lacing and the adoption of shorter skirts, the fashion for short hair and the acceptance of trousers have, since the first decades of the century, made it easier for women to be more active and less circumscribed by their clothes and their appearance. Clothes themselves have become easier to put on and to care for, as women have found less time to devote to the art of dressing and, for the most part, can no longer employ others to help them. The invention of the washing machine, synthetic detergents, coin-operated dry-cleaning machines, the electric iron and the 'easy care' fabrics have helped to make this possible.

At the beginning of the century there was a clear divergence between the clothes of the two sexes. Men's suits presented a uniform appearance and were restricted to sombre colours while women's dresses were feminine in the traditional sense of being shapely, colourful and elaborately trimmed. In following decades the distinction was preserved but, in becoming more practical, women's clothes sometimes emulated or borrowed features from the male wardrobe such as the tailored suit and trousers. In recent decades the tendency towards what is now called 'cross dressing' has become more marked with men and women wearing some garments which appear virtually interchangeable.

Fashion, of course, does not regulate itself to the calendar and respond to the opening of a new year or a new century with a different style or change in direction. In 1900 Queen Victoria was still on the throne and the fashions were those of the late Victorian period. Women's clothes were constructed on the principle of a very firm foundation: a tightly laced and rigidly boned corset to produce as slim a waist and as elegantly rounded a figure as possible. Dresses were made with a separate bodice and skirt, the bodice also firmly boned to preserve the fashionable line. During the first five years of the century this line echoed the sinuous curves of the prevailing *Art Nouveau* taste and it was achieved both by the cut and fall of the dress and by the posture of its wearer. A new type of corset, appearing around 1900, with a long, straight, centre-front busk induced a characteristic S-shaped stance, throwing the bust forward and the hips backwards. Dress bodices and blouses, though they had a rigid understructure, were softly overlaid with material draped in gentle folds over the bust; skirts were fluted in shape to skim the hips and sweep outwards at the hem, with a short train at the back. For daytime wear a full-length, tailored skirt with an elaborately-trimmed, high-necked blouse or a tailored cloth suit and blouse were fashionable. In the evening, dresses were cut with the customary low neckline and short sleeves (or shoulder straps). Materials of a light, airy texture in white, cream or a wide range of pastel colours were usual and were often trimmed with a froth of lace, net, chiffon, beads, ribbons and artificial flowers. Hair was dressed in correspondingly soft, undulating styles, usually over pads to give it the required volume and height, and hats were large with curved brims.

After 1905 this line began to alter, gradually easing out and straightening up so that by 1907–8 there are perceptible signs of a vertical rather than an S-bend silhouette. This was brought about by raising the waistline above its natural level, narrowing the skirt and introducing a new, longer and straighter-fitting corset around 1908. The line was inspired by the short-waisted dresses in the neo-classical taste of the late-eighteenth and early-nineteenth-century period (and was referred to in France as the *Directoire* revival). Paul Poiret, the French designer, although he did not invent this line did much to promote and refine it and by 1909 it was well established. Dress was in effect reflecting a general move away from the softness of *Art Nouveau* taste in the fine and decorative arts and looking towards the hard-edged, geometrical shapes of the Cubist movement.

The neo-classical inspiration at this time was accompanied by a taste for orientalism largely kindled by the sets and costume designs by Léon Bakst for the Russian Ballet. The *Ballets Russes*' first appearances in Paris in 1909 and London in 1911 were regarded as sensational with their exotic and brilliantly coloured images. 'Before one could say Nijinsky', wrote Osbert Lancaster, 'the pale pastel shades which had reigned supreme on the walls of Mayfair for almost two decades were replaced by a riot of barbaric hues – jade green, purple, every variety of crimson and scarlet, and, above all, orange.' (*Homes Sweet Homes*, 1939).

The new tubular line, despite its apparent simplicity, was a particularly restricting form of dress (ironic in view of the fact that the struggle for female emancipation had reached one of its most active stages). The long, slim skirt was cut straight to the ankle with scarcely a flare or vent, making it impossible to take more than the shortest of steps when walking; it was aptly called the 'hobble' skirt and reached its extreme form in 1911–12. At the same time the severity of its line began to be blurred as over-tunics were added and bodices lengthened into jackets; this multiplicity of lengths seemed to be suggesting alternative levels for the hemline and from 1913 the skirt appeared all set to shorten. By the time war broke out in 1914 this idea had crystallized and by 1915 the skirt was several inches above the ankle, widening at the hem to ensure complete freedom of movement. The short skirt was not a creation of the War although the exigencies of war-time no doubt hurried this fashion forward since a more practical form of dress was desirable for women.

In 1915 and 1916 women's fashions made what might be described as a detour from the line so clearly set by 1910. The pillar-like silhouette was abandoned for a more traditionally feminine, even romantic, shape with a wide, bell-shaped skirt which was often flounced. A possible explanation is that this softer, less angular effect was more pleasing to the men returning from the Front who looked for solace while on leave. Towards the end of the War the cylindrical, broad-waisted line was re-adopted and the shorter hemline was retained.

During these years a sharper contrast in the nature of day and evening clothes for women was becoming evident: by day, the practical tailor-made suit with loosely belted jacket and walking skirt, or a tailored dress, in serviceable cloths and colours were preferred while luxury and glamour were concentrated on evening wear. This tendency continued after the War and during the 1920s. Women's clothes for the first time allowed complete freedom of movement and a new sense of ease was further promoted by the adoption of soft, pliable, jersey-knit fabrics for the so-called 'jumper' suits. Chanel, in particular, created comfortable but elegant day clothes for women who wished to look smart but not ostentatious.

The tubular line was not conducive to producing variety and spectacle in evening dresses. From 1920 to 1922 the position of the waistline dropped to the level of the hips, eliminating any shaping over the natural female contours. The fashionable evening dress with low neckline and no sleeves was a virtual tube, requiring little expertise in cut and construction. Consequently it relied largely on surface decoration, the most spectacular the all-over bead embroidery in a myriad of colours and patterns.

The most familiar image of the 1920s – the knee-length, waistless dress worn with a helmet-like cloche hat pulled down to the eyebrows – belongs, in fact, to the later part of the period. Until 1924 the level of the hemline fluctuated, but always around the ankle to mid-calf. Towards the end of that year it began to rise, was noticeably much shorter in 1925 and had reached knee-level in 1926. As the skirt shortened the silhouette began to be pared down so that by 1927 women appeared to be increasingly streamlined. The deep-crowned and narrow-brimmed cloche hat, worn since the beginning of the decade, became severer in shape and fitted the head closely. The neat effect was made possible by cutting the hair short and dressing it close to the head in flat waves. During the 1920s the tubular line was fully explored and perfected but in refining it reduced women almost to a geometric design (like contemporary architecture and furniture the lines were spare, with no projections). This was partly mitigated by the wearing of flamboyant jewellery (pendant earrings, long strings of beads or pearls and large bracelets) and by the use of cosmetics (face powder, lipstick and eyebrow pencil).

By the last two years of the decade the first signs of a reaction against the functional, uncompromising line began to appear. Initial attempts were made to raise the level of the waist and lengthen the skirt while introducing a little more shape and flaring it at the hem. In 1929 the Paris collections showed a gentler line hinting at the natural contours of the bust, waist and hips and by 1930 the new image was complete. As in the later 1920s, the silhouette was smooth and uncluttered but where the emphasis had been on straight, vertical and horizontal lines it was now exploring a soft, supple, diagonal line which could equally well highlight the flatness and slimness of the ideal figure. This new fluidity was achieved by cutting the dress material on the bias or cross-grain of the fabric which gives it more elasticity and draping quality. The technique was by no means new but it was taken up and perfected on a new scale, becoming associated with its greatest exponent in the 1920s and 1930s, the French designer Madeleine Vionnet.

The bias-cut dominated dress design during the first half of the 1930s and was encouraged by a general revival of interest in classical art; evening dresses were especially suitable for recreating the effect of the soft draperies of Antique statuary. By day women's clothes looked neat and disciplined: the potential limpness of the fashion was kept at bay by the careful choice of crisply smart accessories – small hats were tilted at a jaunty angle and clutch bags firmly carried under one arm. The ideal woman was polished and poised.

The long, narrow but fluid line of the earlier 1930s was sharpened and diversified in the second half of the decade. From 1933 the shoulderline was accentuated and widened; towards the end of the thirties the waistline tightened and the hemline rose. By 1938 the trim, tailored suit cut on rather masculine lines seemed to reflect a response to impending war – women's fashion was toughening up. Dress design of the later 1930s was also characterized by elements of eccentricity and fantasy. The first Surrealist Exhibition in London in 1936 may have contributed to a liking for amusing (rather than beautiful) ornaments and patterning; and in France, Elsa Schiaparelli produced a series of lively and original designs. In addition there was a nostalgic revival of late-Victorian and Edwardian fashion with large 'leg-of-mutton' shaped sleeves and full 'crinoline' skirts for romantic evening dresses. Fashion in general was impressed by the glamour of the American film industry which introduced new standards of luxury and display (and encouraged a more positive use of cosmetics).

When the Second World War broke out in 1939 fashion in Britain was more or less frozen for the next five or six years. Cut off from the rest of Europe and in particular from France after it fell to the Germans, British fashion was obliged to look in on itself for inspiration, but was swiftly hampered by government regulations. The need to economize on cloth and other materials essential for the war effort resulted in clothes rationing (in 1941) and the Utility Scheme (which from 1942 strictly governed the design and production of cloth and clothing). These made it impossible to introduce any significant new developments and designers were forced to work within the limited framework of the existing style, either intensifying its characteristic features or making minor alterations to cut and decoration in order to create some variety. The square, padded shoulders, compressed waistline and short skirt length of the late 1930s were thus preserved for the duration of the War. The practical, mannish aspect of these clothes was softened by wearing the hair longer, in more elaborately arranged styles.

With the end of war the fashion industry revived (although in Britain rationing continued until 1949). The French, British and American collections in 1946 showed a general desire for luxury and femininity and there were attempts to introduce longer, fuller skirts and a gentler silhouette. However, it was not until Christian Dior's 'New Look' collection of spring 1947 that these ideas were expressed in a coherent and distinctive form. Dior's look was not really new, in the sense of being completely original, since it was essentially a nostalgic revival of the fashion, last seen in 1915–16, for a slim waist and a wide, ankle-length skirt; but he was able to present it in a different way, combined with a soft, rounded shoulderline and light, pretty footwear in response to the new post-war mood. Other designers followed suit and the line of war-time fashion was quickly rejected.

Although Dior was not the only talented designer working in post-war Paris and was equalled, if not surpassed, by Cristobal Balenciaga, the New Look dominated the shape of fashion in the late 1940s and the first half of the 1950s. Two versions of the fashionable silhouette prevailed: one with the full skirt, the other with a long, straight, slim skirt; but both styles of dress had a fitted bodice, natural shoulderline and slender waist. The general effect was well-tailored and well-groomed, very neat, pretty and feminine, in a studied way. By 1950 short hair had returned and cosmetics (widely available again after the War) were used with enjoyment.

The second half of the decade saw a marked departure from the natural figure line with the most original designs being created in Paris by Balenciaga. The shape of women's dresses became very artificial, the waistline was dropped or raised beyond its normal level, the torso was enlarged in ballooning shapes, collars stood away from the neck, and sleeves were shortened.

Throughout the 1950s the architectural shapes of women's clothes depended on skilful cutting and construction so for Parisian haute couture, which excelled in this, the period was a high point. Towards the end of the decade, however, a new generation of young women were beginning to grow restive under this supremacy. Couture clothes, though beautifully made, were extremely expensive and were mostly designed for the maturer woman; the couturiers were not responding to the increasing trend towards ease and informality in clothes or to the needs of young people (who, with a now more affluent society, had a new purchasing power). In London Mary Quant opened a shop to sell smart, youthful and relatively inexpensive clothes and by the early 1960s several other talented young British designers were following her lead in producing lively and provocative ranges for their own age group.

As in the 1920s, the distinctive style of dress generally associated with the 1960s took some time to evolve and lasted for only a part of the decade. Until 1963, when the hemline just began to rise over the knee-cap, there were few startling changes in women's dress and it was not until 1965 that the new line was fully developed, with the mini-skirt shrinking several inches above the knee. From 1965 to 1968 brief, simple clothes in hard-edged shapes, with little or no ornamentation apart from geometrical patterning, were combined with rigorously geometric hair cuts and stark contrasts in make-up of dark eyes and pale lips. Fashion was inspired by the excitement of new technology, the explorations into Space, Pop and Op Art which all encouraged the use of modern, man-made materials and a liking for white, black and silver. Society appeared to be dominated by the young who were particularly innovative and who also adopted their own kind of universal and classless uniform in the form of blue denim jeans. Even Paris haute couture adapted itself to the new leaders of fashion and young designers like Courrèges and Yves Saint Laurent devoted themselves to a more youthful age group.

The euphoric mood of both optimism and iconoclasm was short-lived and after 1968 it changed direction. Disillusionment or dissatisfaction on the part of many young people with what was seen as a materialistic society led to an 'opting out' or 'dropping out' and the search for an alternative way of life, often through the use of drugs. In dress this was expressed in a general rejection of the assured and rigid line in favour of something softer, more tentative and diffuse. Alternative 'midi' and 'maxi' hem levels were explored, but with some uncertainty, and it was not until about 1974 that the hemline settled again on a generally accepted length covering the knee.

The late 1960s and earlier 1970s saw the flowering of a romantic or fantasy style of dress with the revival of earlier fashions and the borrowing of clothes from other countries and cultures. There was, for example, a liking for Victorian- and Edwardian-inspired long skirts, frilled blouses and laced boots (especially in the work of Laura Ashley) and original specimens of these clothes, found in antique markets and junk shops, were also worn. Long, loose, Indian, Far Eastern and South American garments and jewellery were adopted, first by the 'Hippy' movement and later absorbed into the mainstream of fashion.

The influence of the Far East was felt in other ways and in the mid-to-late 1970s Japanese dress designers in Paris were making an impact on high fashion, challenging the established shape and cut of Western clothing by introducing features of the wrapped, layered and untailored styles of traditional oriental dress; but it was several years before these ideas passed into common currency.

The most original and dynamic contribution to stylistic development in the 1970s came paradoxically from the negative, anarchic 'Punk' movement which was essentially subversive and anti-style. In the later 1970s a minority of young people reacted violently to a conformist society which seemed to offer them nothing, by deliberately and perversely cultivating the bizarre, the ugly and the shocking. Hair was dyed and sculpted into spiky, menacing forms, faces were painted and noses and ears pierced with safety pins, black tattered clothes were punctuated with metal studs and zips and shackled with chains and straps. The intention was to reject fashion and its conventions, though fashion itself responded by absorbing and modifying many of these elements. The influence of the Punk movement and 'street fashion' has extended to the early 1980s and its most significant result has probably been a general questioning of the conventional ideas of femininity and status in women's clothes.

Another line of thought which affected fashion in the late 1970s and early 1980s has been an intense interest in physical fitness. Not only has this encouraged the design of new ranges of sportswear for men and women but it has also changed the emphasis in dress design. Unlike the 1950s when clothes imposed the shape of fashion on a woman, garments have in recent years tended to take their line from the wearer. Longer, looser, unstructured clothes, in the manner of drapery, can be designed to reveal and enhance the natural shape and contours of the human body – although to be most effective, the body needs to be slim and fit (without the artificial aid of structural underwear). A relaxed, indefinite shaping of clothes can also serve to blur the distinctions between male and female dress and this too has been a feature of the early 1980s, with even a minority cult of male transvestism; but in general it is women's clothes which have drawn closer to men's rather than the reverse.

In comparision with the variety and continual change in women's dress during the present century, men's clothes have appeared uniform and unvarying in character. The three-piece lounge suit of 1900 is very similar in form to its modern version although there are differences in cut, shape, material and decoration; the morning coat, evening dress suit and dinner jacket, though less commonly worn now, still feature in the contemporary male wardrobe with little significant alteration. Nevertheless, over eight decades changes have occurred and the fashionable male silhouette, like its female counterpart, has been re-shaped from one projected ideal to another within its somewhat conservative and limited framework. In the 1960s there was a marked revival of interest in the design of men's clothes (sometimes referred to as the 'Peacock Revolution') and many established conventions regarding, for example, the use of colour, shapes and forms of male clothing were challenged.

When the century opened men's dress was generally formal and carefully regulated according to a man's occupation and the time of day. The frock coat and morning suit were correct for day wear, with the three-piece lounge suit as an alternative for less formal occasions in town and for country wear. The appropriate accessories (shirt collar, necktie, hat, gloves and shoes) underlined the degree of formality. In the evening the dress suit with tail coat, white waistcoat and white bow tie was usual for formal functions while the dinner suit (an evening version of the lounge suit, worn with a black bow tie and waistcoat) was worn at other times. The cut of the suit was fairly narrow and there was a general air of neatness and a certain amount of inflexibility – shirt collars were high and well starched. Edward VII, who was personally interested in clothes and the etiquette of dress, set a high standard of male elegance during the first decade of the century.

The second decade was dominated by the First World War which drew attention away from civilian men's dress and it was not until the 1920s that new developments became apparent. As with women's dress, there was an unmistakable air of greater ease and mobility after the ending of war with a general trend towards more informality during the 1920s and 1930s. The shirt collar was lowered and gradually the stiff, winged style was replaced by a soft, turned-down collar; the frock coat, so much associated with the late Victorian period, passed out of fashion and the morning suit was relegated to more formal wear. Professional and business men wore single- or double-breasted, three-piece lounge suits during the day and other forms of casual dress took their place for informal wear. The tweed sports jacket (adapted from the riding or hacking jacket) or the blazer (originally worn for yachting or by the sea) with flannel trousers were usual in the country and at week-ends; golfing clothes (a rough tweed knickerbocker suit and a knitted pullover) were also taken up for ordinary wear.

By the mid-1920s the shape of the male suit had changed quite considerably. Trousers which had previously been narrow and tapered now widened (known in their most extreme form as 'Oxford Bags') and the jacket widened at the shoulder and loosened at the waist to become much squarer in shape. The slacker fit and more geometrical line echoed similar developments in the female silhouette. In the 1930s there was a parallel emphasis on the slimness and flatness of the hips, accentuated by the width of the shoulders. The cut of the male jacket became increasingly boxy in shape, accentuated by shoulder padding, wide lapels and the double-breasted fastening which was particularly fashionable. Trouser legs corresponded in shape by being cut wide with turn-ups at the hem. Knitted waistcoats, sleeveless pullovers and sweaters were popular informal wear.

Once again, the outbreak of war in 1939 put a stop to any progress in male fashion and during the Second World War men's clothes were rationed and restricted by Utility regulations (new suits were allowed only a certain number of pockets and buttons, had single-breasted jackets and trousers no wider than 19 inches with no turn-ups). The square, loose cut prevailed to the end of the 1940s and in America became more exaggerated, with the jacket hanging loosely from a wide shoulderline in what was called the 'drape', while trousers were pleated into the front of the waistband to give the required width in the leg.

By 1950 the British fashion industry had re-established itself, men demobilized from the armed services were needing new civilian clothes, and there was a renewed interest in their design. In the same way that women were rejecting the war-time line in favour of something softer and more fitted, men's suits began to narrow down as the shoulders and legs gradually lost their excessive width. A minority of well-off and fashion-conscious young men pursued a new ideal of elegance which was compared with the lean lines and exquisite tailoring of the early years of the century and they were called the 'neo-Edwardians'; the name and some of these ideas were then transformed into the distinctive new working-class style of dress of the Teddy Boys, with their long jackets, narrow 'drainpipe' trousers and jeans, bootlace ties and heavy crêpe-soled shoes. It was an image which came to be associated with a whole new culture for teenagers in the 1950s along with rock and roll music, juke boxes and coffee bars. Other teenage cults (often with a working-class basis) were to follow and the Mods and Rockers were to dominate the first half of the 1960s.

During the 1950s and early 1960s there was a progressive paring down of the male silhouette. Suits tended increasingly towards a narrower cut with slimmer trousers and more fitted jackets which had a natural shoulderline, smaller lapels and the single-breasted fastening. This trend owed much to the influence of Italian designers and the so-called 'Italian suit', rather tightly and sharply cut in light cloths, was greatly admired. New developments in the production of man-made fibres resulted in lighter-weight and crease-resistant suitings and drip-dry shirts which added to the new, neat, well-pressed look of men's clothes. It was further emphasized by the spiky appearance of fashionable footwear, now much lighter with longer, pointed toes. Even teenagers followed this line: jeans were straight and very narrow in cut and combined with 'winklepicker' shoes. In reaction to the rather fashion-conscious Mods, the Rockers of the earlier 1960s affected a tougher, 'motor-bike' dress with the addition of studded leather jackets and longer, greased hair.

In the 1960s male fashion was given an injection of vitality when in London, in particular, new ranges of inexpensive and vibrant clothes were produced for young men and sold in the new boutiques (the most famous of which were located in the King's Road and Carnaby Street). These were not especially well made but were often inventive, experimenting with materials, colours and patterns until then considered impossible in the male wardrobe. Much of the impetus and inspiration for these styles came from the pop groups, led by the Beatles and the Rolling Stones. At the couture level the French designer, Pierre Cardin, made an important contribution to the production of youthful and stylish clothes for men.

In the late 1960s the Hippy movement took the line of experiment further, encouraging the adoption of ethnic clothing (especially Indian garments), long robes, beads and long hair. Flowers, the Hippy symbol of peace and love, were transferred to the patterning of even quite conventional garments such as shirt and ties. The form of men's clothes remained much the same, however: the two-piece suit was still usual for formal day wear and the sports jacket and trousers continued to be worn by most ordinary men. Innovations lay in the altered cut of trousers, flaring them at the hem in the late 1960s (a style which continued well into the 1970s) and also of shirts and ties – shirts became skin-tight with long, pointed or rounded collars and ties were enlarged to the fashionable kipper shape. But throughout the 1960s the most characteristic garment for teenagers, students and other young people were denim jeans (worn with T-shirts or sweaters and running shoes). It was a cheap, practical yet stylish form of dress, both classless and a badge of freedom from convention.

Casual wear was becoming increasingly important and by the early 1970s it was receiving attention from the international couture designers (Yves Saint Laurent, for example, started his ready-to-wear ranges for men as well as women) taking it beyond the limits of jeans, open-necked shirts, crew-necked sweaters and casual jackets. Blouson jackets, ribbed polo-necked sweaters, styled cloth trousers with pleated fronts and wider legs (a revival of the thirties style) were all introduced. A tougher element and alternative style of dress continued to emerge from the youth on the streets – most notably the Skinheads (of the late 1960s and early 1970s) with their short crewcuts, collarless shirts, braces, ankle-short trousers and 'bovver' boots, and later in the 1970s the Punks who were making a stand against status and the establishment.

Apart from the emphasis on informal wear and separates, clothes for more conventional men in the later 1970s settled back, for the most part, into a pattern of classic styles in subdued colours with undramatic modifications in cut and styling from season to season. The early 1980s has nevertheless seen a revival of interest in male fashion but designers have been exploring a new direction, moving from the established, structured nature of men's garments towards new concepts of shape and fit.

A general survey of the twentieth century, up to the time of writing, is inevitably both selective and subjective. The wealth of information and visual images is enormous and, because we are living through the period, we are ourselves far more acutely aware of the subtle meanings of contemporary fashion than we would be when reading the language of clothes of an earlier century. In making a choice of illustrations to trace the most important stylistic developments during this period it is necessary to leave some aspects out or to mention them only briefly; it is impossible to cover every type of dress from the most fashionable to the most ordinary, of every age group, social class and occupation and to examine in detail the related aspects of underclothing and children's fashions. These aspects have been referred to but a work of this size cannot hope to be completely comprehensive. In addition, although this survey is intended mainly as a guide to the development of dress in twentieth-century Britain some illustrations of influential French, Italian, American and Japanese designers have been included.

Obviously many of the original garments from this era are still surviving in near perfect condition and can be viewed in museum displays and exhibitions. This is excellent in order to appreciate the look of the garment itself, its shape and proportion, its material and decoration in three dimensions; as a source of information, original specimens are essential to the study of twentieth-century dress. At the same time, museums are limited in the way they can present such an object, for however well mounted it is, on as naturalistic a mannequin as possible, it is still a static figure and, as often as not, in a glass case. The museum display can only suggest how the garment might have looked when it was worn. To appreciate what the wearer looked like in such clothes, how the clothes behaved and how they affected the wearer's posture and gestures, how they related to the other dress accessories and how well they expressed the fashionable ideal, it is necessary to look at contemporary illustrations. In the present century there is a wide range of closely dated visual evidence to draw upon: paintings, portraits, drawings, engravings, cartoons, book illustrations, posters, sculpture, photographs, fashion plates, advertisements and trade catalogues (not to mention the further dimension of ciné film, the cinema and television). It is to these sources that we can look to appreciate most clearly the fashionable silhouette and style of beauty favoured in each decade and to give us an impression of that elusive and indescribable element, the 'atmosphere' of a period.

Although photography was invented some 60 years before the century began, its full potential was not realized until later and rather surprisingly, photography only began to be widely used to illustrate fashion from around 1900. Since then fashion photography has developed as a separate field and provides a continuous, accurate and invaluable source of visual information on high fashion during the twentieth century. Most of these photographs have become available in the form of published illustrations in newspapers and magazines but some archives of the original photographs are now housed in museums. Photography has gradually replaced the traditional methods of fashion illustration although drawings and sketches are still used to some extent today. The engraved plate, lithograph or print, often coloured by hand, had little life beyond the 1920s but during the first three decades of the century it was still used to illustrate the more expensive fashion periodicals and indeed underwent a brief revival of the art with the exquisite pochoir prints used for the *Gazette du Bon Ton*, *Art Goût Beauté*, and *Journal des Dames et des Modes*. Fashion plates, drawings and sometimes even fashion photographs have the disadvantage, as a source of information, in stressing the ideal image (often to the point of distortion) at the expense of reality; therefore they need to be used with care, balanced by illustrations whose visual reporting, so to speak, is more straightforward. Into this category fall the many other photographs which are available: professional studio portraits, press photographs, amateur snapshots and family groups – of most value if they are firmly dated.

The widespread use of photography contributed to, though was not wholly responsible for, the decline of the painted, drawn or sculpted portrait in the twentieth century. Portraits, genre paintings, drawings, engravings and sculpture though still an important source of visual evidence for the study of dress in this period have not been used quite as extensively in this book as in the preceding volumes of the series, partly to balance the claims of other visual sources and partly because of problems peculiar to the present century. The steady move away from representational painting and sculpture towards more abstract and conceptual forms of art since the first decade of the century has meant that for the historian of dress there are fewer works of art on which to draw for a realistic depiction of people's appearance and clothing. The art of portrait painting has by no means died out but the number of sitters who are either rich enough or important enough to have their portraits painted is relatively small and they represent a narrow sector of society. It is also the case that a number of paintings and portraits by twentieth-century artists are still in private collections and are not always accessible to many members of the public.

There are comparatively few examples of twentieth-century sculpture which can be used as a source of information to students of dress although the realistic and fully-dressed fibreglass figures of the American artist Duane Hanson and others in the last decade or so provide an interesting record of clothing in another medium. One minor but significant branch of the art of sculpture should also be considered, the shop-window display mannequin, a twentieth-century phenomenon. Like the fashion illustration these reveal the aspirations of a period – the facial features and shape of body, even a style of posture, generally admired. A few examples, with their original wigs and make-up, contemporary with the clothes they are displaying, have been included in the illustrations.

New techniques of printing and reproduction (such as cheap, coloured prints and the half-tone illustration) have made a wider range of visual material available during this century and these can be useful sources to supplement and counterbalance those which are more directly concerned with making statements about fashion. A selection of these can be found in this survey to represent other areas that can be explored, such as illustrations to books and magazines, shop catalogues and advertisements.

This book deals with only part of a century and with the dress of our own time without the benefit of hindsight. It is hoped that, incomplete as it is, it may serve as a tail-piece to the *Visual History of Costume* until the remaining history of our century can be written.

1 Men's Fashions, 1900
Anon. engraving

Note *The Tailor and Cutter* shows the three fashionable styles of day suits for men at the beginning of the century: morning suit (left), frock coat (centre) and lounge suit (right).

Head The hair is cut short and close to the head. Facial hair is passing out of fashion and although moustaches are still worn by some men, side-whiskers are no longer seen.

Body The morning coat (left) has a single-breasted fastening and slopes back at the sides to form tails at the back; the waistcoat is single-breasted and the rather narrow trousers are cut long (to break over the shoe). The shirt has a high, starched, 'wing' or 'butterfly' collar and the necktie is long and knotted. The dark frock coat

(centre) is knee-length, with straight front edges, long lapels and double-breasted fastening. It is worn with a double-breasted waistcoat with a deep shawl collar, and light-coloured trousers. The shirt has a high, stiff, 'double' or turned-over collar and narrow bow tie. The lounge suit (right) has a short, single-breasted jacket, waistcoat and trousers to match, with starched wing collar and long, knotted tie. After the 1890s the centre crease in the trouser leg became usual.

Accessories The formal top hat is worn with the frock coat and morning suit; a Homburg (a soft felt hat with ribbon-bound brim) is teamed with the more informal lounge suit. All three men either wear or carry gloves and have a walking stick or rolled umbrella. The men in morning suit and frock coat have flowers in their buttonholes while the man in the lounge suit wears a folded handkerchief in his breast pocket. Their laced shoes are narrow with pointed toes.

2 Boer War 1900 (detail)
J. B. L. Shaw

Note The title and the woman's black clothes suggest she is in mourning for a husband or relative killed in the war in South Africa. She is holding a hank of knitting yarn in purple, another traditional mourning colour.

Head The hair is long, drawn back from the face from a centre parting and coiled round the back of the head.

Body She is wearing day dress, consisting of a separate bodice and skirt. The bodice, striped in black and white, has a high neck-band, fashionable at this date, and long sleeves which are cut with fullness at the top of the arm – a lingering but modified version of the leg-of-mutton shaped sleeve popular in the mid-1890s. The plain black, full-length skirt is gored to flare at the hem and her narrow waist is accentuated by a tightly-buckled belt.

Accessories A long thin gold chain with a pendant hangs from her neck to well below the waist (this type of necklace was known as a *sautoir* chain). She has a gold *châtelaine* attached to her belt (a series of chains suspending objects such as a watch, pencil, needlework accessories, keys etc.).

3 The Sisters, 1900
R. Peacock

Note Fashionable day wear for young women growing up at the turn of the century. The practical tailored skirt and blouse with masculine collar and tie had become popular in the 1890s and continued to be worn throughout the Edwardian period. Although the sisters are similarly dressed the difference in their age and status is marked by the way their hair is dressed. Young girls wore their hair long and loose until they left the schoolroom, then put their hair up when they 'came out' in society.

Head The elder sister's hair is rolled back from the face and coiled round the back of the head; the younger's falls loosely to waist level.

Body Both girls wear striped blouses with long sleeves; the high necklines are finished with white, turned-down collars and neckties (on the left, a spotted, fringed scarf tied in a bow, on the right, a long, knotted tie). Their skirts are long and plain, widening towards the hem and belted at the waist.

Accessories The elder sister wears an elaborately wrought silver belt buckle.

4 Ball dress, 1900
C. Drivon

Note This fashion plate from *The Queen* exaggerates, to the point of distortion, the lines of the ideal figure at this moment: tall and stately with a full bust, very narrow waist and slim hips.

Head The model's long hair is arranged in a chignon at the back of the head; at the front it is teased out in a curled fringe.

Body She wears a formal evening gown comprising a separate bodice and skirt. The bodice is very low-cut with narrow shoulder straps; the material is softly swathed across the bust but is mounted on a very firm understructure. The skirt is tulip-shaped, fitting closely round the waist and hips but flaring at the hem to extend into a short train.

Accessories Long white kid gloves, a folding ostrich-feather fan, hair ornament, corsage, waist ornament and bracelets complete the dress.

5 The Family of George Campbell Swinton at Pont Street, London, 1901
W. Orpen

Note The sitters are Elizabeth Ebsworth, Mrs Swinton; Mary Swinton (later Lady William Percy); Alan Henry Campbell Swinton and George Campbell Swinton. Orpen's portrait appears as a mirror-reflection on the wall. The fashionable cut of Mrs Swinton's dress, the elaborate nature of the children's clothes and the quiet but well-tailored elegance of their father suggest that this is a well-to-do family. Mrs Swinton's confident pose with her hand on one hip (which incidentally draws attention to the narrowness of her waist) was a favourite stance at this period (see also no. 13).

Head Although they are indoors both Mrs Swinton and her infant daughter wear hats. Mrs Swinton's has a wide, curved brim trimmed with ostrich feathers; her little girl's has a deep crown and wide brim. Mr Swinton's hair is parted at the centre and he has a long moustache.

Body Mrs Swinton's day dress has a V-shaped opening with turned-back collar filled in with a high-necked dress front. Her flounced skirt is cut with additional fullness at the back to form a short train. Mr Swinton wears a dark frock coat with lighter-coloured waistcoat and trousers; his shirt has a stiff, double collar. Mary Swinton is dressed in a flounced coat and dress, her brother in a shirt with a wide collar and knee-breeches.

7 Ena and Betty, Daughters of Asher and Mrs Wertheimer, 1901
J. S. Sargent

See colour plate, between pp. 120 and 121.

8 The Return from the Ride, 1902
C. W. Furse

Note The sitters, Aubrey and Lina Waterfield, married in 1901. It is known that Mrs Waterfield is wearing her 'going-away' dress for this picture although it is an idealized portrait in which she appears as a highly romantic figure recalling images of an earlier century. There was a considerable revival of interest in the art and fashions of the later-eighteenth century at this time and in this portrait the artist has exaggerated certain features of her dress (the large hat, the width of her skirt and her floating scarf) to suggest the effect of perhaps a Gainsborough lady.

Head Mrs Waterfield's hair is long and dressed from a centre parting beneath her large-brimmed hat and veil. It was fashionable at this date for the brim of the hat to curve upwards and forwards. Mr Waterfield's hair is cut short and he is clean shaven.

Body Her dress, made of silk, has a full skirt and long, ruffled sleeves; she wears a thin muslin scarf or fichu over her shoulders. He is in riding clothes: short jacket, jodhpurs and riding boots. His shirt has a soft, turned-down collar and his necktie is knotted in a bow with long ends.

Accessories The man's wide-brimmed hat is of fine straw with a ribbon band.

6 Afternoon dress by Paquin, 1901
Photograph by Reutlinger

Note A semi-formal dress for summer afternoon wear of *broderie anglaise* and Valenciennes lace, photographed for the French fashion magazine, *Les Modes*. Photographs were now beginning to replace the traditional fashion drawings and engravings to illustrate the latest styles.

Head The model's long hair is swept off her face and rolled back softly over pads, the remainder twisted into a knot on the top of the head, in the fashionable 'cottage loaf' style.

Body The dress has a high-necked bodice with elbow-length sleeves and full under-sleeves gathered into deep cuffs at the wrist; extra fullness across the bust gives a soft, pouched effect over a deep and very tightly-fitting waistband. The skirt is cut straight at the front with added fullness at the back extending into a train. The general effect is one of softly undulating curves in the S-bend shape.

9 Madame Réjane in a tea gown by Doucet, 1902
Anon. photograph

Note Couture clothes were often modelled by stage actresses and singers for the leading fashion magazines such as *Les Modes* in the early years of the century.

Head Her hair is arranged in waves across her forehead and pinned up at the back.

Body She wears a diaphanous tea gown of finely pleated chiffon trimmed with lace. The tea gown was a loose-fitting, informal garment worn by ladies in the late afternoon before dressing for dinner and it was particularly fashionable in the period from the 1890s to 1914. Although beautifully and elaborately made in the most delicate of fabrics the tea gown was primarily a garment in which to relax and it afforded a welcome opportunity to dispense with tightly laced corsets for a short time during the day. However, it could also be worn as an informal dinner dress (over the usual underwear and corset) and in this example Madame Réjane's tightly-constricted waist is clearly visible beneath the transparent fabric of her gown.

10 General Sir Frederick Forestier-Walker, 1902
L. Ward

Note One of the many portraits of distinguished men painted by 'Spy' for the magazine *Vanity Fair*.

Head The General wears his hair cut short and brushed back from his brow; he has no side-whiskers but a fairly long moustache.

Body He wears a dark cloth frock coat with wide lapels faced with silk and a double-breasted fastening; his waistcoat is single-breasted and has a white 'slip' visible at the top edge; the trousers are of grey striped cloth. His shirt has a high, stiff collars and he wears a long, knotted tie. In the later Victorian period the frock coat was the usual formal day wear for gentlemen but by the early years of the twentieth century it was becoming less fashionable (though still correct).

Accessories A jewelled pin can be seen just below the knot of his necktie and he wears a watch chain across his waistcoat.

11 Seaside wear, 1902
G. L. Stampa

Note The man and woman in this *Punch* cartoon wear informal day clothes at a seaside resort. The man has a relaxed air with his pipe in one hand and the other in his pocket. The woman's stance, with hands folded and leaning slightly on her parasol is characteristic of this period.

Head The man's hair is cut very short and he is clean shaven. The woman's long hair is knotted at the nape of her neck. Both wear straw hats – the man a boater and the woman a large hat trimmed with artificial flowers.

Body The man has on an easy-fitting lounge jacket with narrow lapels and single-breasted fastening, and light-coloured trousers. His shirt collar is stiffened in the wing or butterfly style with a long, knotted tie. The woman wears a blouse and long, tailored skirt. The blouse has a wide collar trimmed with braid and the opening is filled in, high to the neck; although it appears easy-fitting the blouse would have been worn over a rigidly boned corset.

Accessories Gloves are worn by the woman and she carries a parasol or umbrella with a long handle and striped cover.

12 Wedding group, 1903
Photograph by Weber

Note A group of guests of different ages at a middle-class wedding.

Head All the men have short hair parted at one side. Some are clean shaven and some wear moustaches; only the clergyman (centre) has a full beard. All the women wear hats or bonnets, the younger women in fashionably large hats with big brims elaborately trimmed, and the older ladies in smaller, closer-fitting headdresses reminiscent of the late Victorian period.

Body The men are dressed in frock coats but show a variety of collars and neckties. The bride and her bridesmaids wear finely pin-tucked and flounced dresses trimmed with ribbon rosettes. Many of the other ladies wear the tailored costume (a cloth jacket and skirt) with a high-necked blouse which had become fashionable for formal day wear.

Accessories Hats, gloves and floral buttonholes are worn by most of the guests. Several ladies wear pearl choker necklaces.

13 Violet and Gold (also called *L'Entente Cordiale*), 1905
J. Lavery

Note The elegant and fashionable appearance of the sitter's clothes together with her confident stance place her in the upper levels of society. Although the bodice is still cut with a certain amount of fullness over the bust it is now evident that the silhouette is beginning to alter: the exaggerated S-bend shape of the figure is straightening out and the waistline is on the point of rising.

Head The sitter's long hair is drawn back from a centre parting in a softly-rounded style.

Body She is wearing a three-piece costume of matching bolero jacket and skirt with a white blouse. The short bolero jacket was a very fashionable garment at this date. The blouse has a high neck-band and long sleeves, full in the upper arm but tight towards the wrist.

Accessories A small brooch is visible in the neck-band of the blouse and she wears a ring.

14 American sisters presented at the Court of Edward VII, *c*.1905
Lafayette

Note A photograph of the beautiful Mrs Arthur Lee (later Viscountess Lee of Fareham) and her sister, Miss Faith Moore, in their Court Presentation dresses. Attendance at court marked a young woman's debut into Society and the rules governing the correct dress for presentations to the monarch were strict. Full evening dress (white for debutantes) was usual with the addition of a headdress of white feathers and tulle veil, long white gloves, a large bouquet of flowers, and a fan.

Head Both sisters wear their long hair rolled back over pads in a soft, round style. The customary three white ostrich feathers for Court wear are fixed to the crown of their heads. Originally a plume of several feathers was worn but by the early years of the century the number had been reduced to three (symbolizing the Prince of Wales's emblem) and by 1912 these were being worn slightly to the left-hand side of the head.

Body They wear elaborate and formal evening dresses with low, round necklines and short sleeves; the bodice and skirts are lavishly embroidered and trimmed as are the separate trains (attached to the dress at either the waist or shoulders) which were obligatory for attendance at Court.

Accessories They hold large, round, be-ribboned bouquets and wear necklaces and brooches. The other usual Court dress accessories – long white gloves and fans – are not visible in this picture.

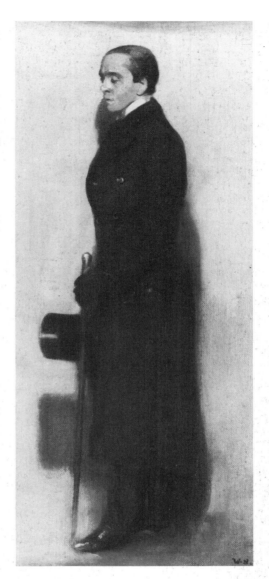

15 Sir Max Beerbohm, 1905
W. Nicholson

Note Max Beerbohm (1872–1956), the author and cartoonist, was a noted dandy and one of the few men to praise the costume of his time. He commended 'its sombre delicacy, its congruities of black and white and grey' and the way it produced 'a supreme effect through means the least extravagant'.

Head His hair is short and very neat, being smoothed flat over the crown.

Body He wears a long, fitted, Chesterfield overcoat in dark cloth. His shirt collar is high and stiff.

Accessories He carries a top hat and walking stick and wears gloves.

AUTO SLIP-ON

AUTOMO
WEATHER-ALL

AUTO-WEATHER-ALL, WITH CAPE

16 Ladies' automobile clothes by Burberry's, c. 1905
Anon. engraving

Note As motor cars came into use in the early years of the century, special protective clothing was introduced for both men and women.

Head All three ladies protect their hair with large and rather flat-crowned hats. The model on the right has added a long motoring veil covering the hat, face and neck.

Body The three coats are long and full to give overall protection against cold, wet and dust while travelling in an open motor car. They are made of fairly heavy, waterproofed cloth with a fleece lining and are cut to fit comfortably over several layers of clothing. The deep collars can be turned up or down.

Accessories Gauntlet gloves are worn.

17 Holiday Crowds, Waterloo, 15 September 1906
'F.D.'

Note A group of travellers of different ages, social classes and occupations.

Head Every person in this picture is wearing a hat of some kind. The men (including cab drivers) wear top hats or the less formal bowler, trilby and flat cap. A wide-brimmed clerical hat can be seen to the right of centre. The younger women are in hats while some elderly ladies are wearing the older-fashioned bonnets.

Body Many of the people, as might be expected, are in travelling or sporting clothes. The man on the extreme left is dressed for golf and a young woman with a bicycle wears a tailored jacket and skirt with masculine shirt, tie and flat cap. The woman in the centre has a full-length, loose-fitting overcoat and the two little boys with her wear a sailor suit (left) and a Norfolk suit (right). The railway porter on the far right is in the common uniform of short jacket, waistcoat and trousers with a white shirt collar, dark tie and peaked cap. The characteristic peaked cap (similar in shape to the military forage cap) had been adopted by railway company staff in the mid-nineteenth century.

Accessories The importance of umbrellas and walking sticks is shown by the number of examples carried by travellers and the collection in the foreground strapped up in travelling rugs.

18 Society's Saturday: Tea on the Lawn outside the Club-House at Ranelagh, 1907
Simone

Note An engraving from *The Illustrated London News* illustrating one of the fashionable social events of the London Season.

Head Women's hats are becoming noticeably deeper in the crown and hair arrangements are rounder and fuller. The men all wear the formal top hat.

Body A silk dress with a light scarf or shoulder cape was the usual wear for a formal afternoon function of this kind. There is a change in the fashionable silhouette for women as the waistline rises and the skirt becomes straighter and narrower. The men wear frock coats with striped trousers and high, starched shirt collars with cravats.

Accessories The women either wear or carry gloves. The two in the foreground (left) display a number of rings and bracelets. The men carry walking sticks.

19 Three gowns by Paul Poiret, 1908
P. Iribe

Note Paul Poiret (1879–1944) was one of the most influential French fashion designers in the first two decades of the century. His work was stylishly publicized in 1908 by the illustrations of Paul Iribe in a *de luxe* booklet called *Les robes de Paul Poiret*. His designs were notable for their elegance and economy of line.

Head The women's hair arrangements are stylized in this illustration but suggest the neo-classical inspiration with their loose curls and Grecian-type fillets.

Body The dresses are extremely simple and severe in shape with the raised waistline and straight, tubular skirt reminiscent of the neo-classical taste of the early-nineteenth-century period. The natural curves of the female figure have been almost entirely eliminated and there is a marked absence of ornament – the decoration of these gowns is handled with restraint and an almost geometrical precision. Poiret's colour range was bold and brilliant, rejecting the soft, pretty pastel shades popular at the turn of the century.

20 Day dresses by Harrods, 1909
Anon. print

Note The early years of the century saw the heyday of the great London department stores and Harrods, among others, produced regular, lavishly illustrated catalogues of goods on sale.

Head Most of the men wear top hats (the correct accessory to a frock coat or morning coat) but one can be seen in a bowler (worn with a lounge suit). The women's hats are all large, with deep crowns and wide brims, heavily trimmed.

Body Although one man (centre left) wears a morning coat and one (far right) is in a frock coat, a third (right) can be seen in the less formal lounge suit which was becoming increasingly popular for day wear in town. Some of the women wear long coats over their day dresses. The fashionable line continues to narrow as the waistline rises and the skirt contracts. However, there is still a liking for applied ornament and clothes are trimmed with embroidery, braid and decorative buttons.

Accessories The lady in the centre carries a small drawstring hand bag, known as a 'Dorothy' bag and popular at this date.

32

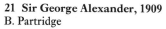

21 Sir George Alexander, 1909
B. Partridge

Note The famous actor-manager is portrayed in formal evening dress.

Head His hair is a little longer than was conventional at this date but would have been acceptable in view of the artistic nature of his profession.

Body He wears an evening suit with a cut-in tail coat or 'dress' coat and matching trousers of fine, black wool cloth, with a white waistcoat. The dress coat was cut away in a horizontal line across the waist (as opposed to sloping back at the sides as in the swallow-tailed morning coat). A white waistcoat was now customary with the dress suit rather than the black one preferred during the Victorian period. A white shirt with starched front, stiff wing collar and white bow tie were correct accessories to formal evening dress. Links fastening his shirt cuffs are also visible at his wrists.

22 Evening dress by Lucile, *c.* 1910
Fashion illustration

Note Lucile (Lucy Kennedy, later Lady Duff Gordon, 1862–1935) was a talented London couturier who was one of the first British designers to be considered equal to the great French fashion houses. She was particularly noted for her diaphanous gowns in light fabrics and pretty colours.

Head The hair is still long but it is now dressed closer to the head which appears smaller and neater.

Body Her long black silk evening dress is covered with a slanted tunic of black beaded and fringed net; it has a low, square neck opening and short sleeves. The bodice is short-waisted and the skirt narrow with a short train in the fashionable revival of the style of dress worn in the early-nineteenth century. In France this was referred to as the *Directoire* revival (i.e. recalling the fashions during the French *Directoire* period of government from 1795 to 1799).

23 Horace Annesley Vachell, *c.* **1910**
G. Linden

Note Horace Annesley Vachell (1861–1955) was the author of over 50 novels and fourteen plays. He is dressed here in informal summer clothes.

Head His hair is cut short with no side-whiskers and he wears a moustache.

Body Vachell's suit consists of a matching lounge jacket and double-breasted waistcoat in a light, textured tweed, worn with white trousers. His shirt has a starched turned-down collar and he wears a narrow, dark, knotted tie.

Accessories Under one arm he hold a soft, light Panama straw hat with striped silk hat band (a style which was replacing the boater for summer wear); the other hand, holding a cigarette, rests on a walking stick. A watch chain is worn across his waistcoat.

24 The Children of George V, 1910
W. & O. Downey

Note The children are: back row left to right –
Prince Albert (later George VI), Princess Mary
(Princess Royal and Countess of Harewood),
Prince Edward (Edward VIII and Duke of
Windsor); front row left to right – Prince John,
Prince Henry (Duke of Gloucester), Prince
George (Duke of Kent). Their clothes reflect the
formal style of dress worn by children in the
Edwardian period.

Head The boys all wear their hair cut short and
parted on the left side. Princess Mary's hair is long
and brushed back in loose, natural curls.

Body The two elder boys (back row) wear the
uniform of Royal Naval cadets; two of the younger
ones are in the sailor suits still fashionable for
small boys and Prince Henry (centre) is in another
popular style, the Eton suit with wide, turned-
back shirt collar. Princess Mary's white-
embroidered dress is high-necked and long-
sleeved with a short skirt reaching to just below
the knee; with it she wears white stockings and
plain court shoes with pointed toes and low heels.

25 The Jester (W. Somerset Maugham), 1911
G. Kelly

Note One of many portraits Kelly painted of the
writer William Somerset Maugham (1874–1965).
He is portrayed here as an elegant figure, formally
dressed, in an opulent setting.

Head His hair is very neatly trimmed and hardly
visible beneath his grey top hat. He wears a thick
moustache.

Body Maugham is dressed in a dark morning suit
with a white, stiffened, turned-down shirt collar
and dark tie.

Accessories There is a white handkerchief in the
breast pocket of his coat and he wears light-
coloured gloves. His laced shoes are of plain black
leather. He holds a walking stick with crook
handle.

26 Tailored costume from *Chic Parisien*, 1911
Anon. lithograph

Note The French *Directoire* revival included elements of both eighteenth- and early-nineteenth-century dress, sometimes borrowing features from the male wardrobe. This jacket with its sloped sides is clearly inspired by the male riding coat of the 1790s while the high neck-band and jabot of the blouse recall the man's stock and shirt ruffle of the mid-eighteenth century. Her buckled shoes are also reminiscent of the footwear of that period (though these were actually called 'Cromwell' shoes).

Head By 1911 hats had become extremely large with deep, mushroom-shaped crowns and wide brims; by surmounting an increasingly slim, straight figure they created an almost T-shaped silhouette. Width on the head was also emphasized in the arrangement of the hair which was waved over the ears.

Body Her tailored cloth costume has a short jacket with its high waist accentuated by a belt, and a long, narrow skirt. Since these new, slim skirts did not widen towards the hem they were difficult to walk in and were aptly called 'hobble' skirts.

Accessories She wears long white gloves and holds a long, very tightly furled parasol or umbrella.

27 Oranges and Lemons, 1911
H. Willebeek Le Mair

Note This illustration from a children's book, *Our Old Nursery Rhymes*, shows how closely the style of young girls' clothes reflected adult fashions at this date. The new line (publicized in France by Paul Poiret in 1908) encouraged the adoption of lighter, less elaborate dresses for little girls compared with the formality of the Edwardian period (see no. 5). From this time onwards there was to be more freedom in children's clothes.

Head The little girls all have long or shoulder-length hair. Almost every child, including the baby, wears a hat. Several of the hats are of the fashionable 'cloche' or 'thimble' shape with a deep crown and no brim; there is also an example of the 'Napoleon' or 'bicorne' hat (right of centre) with the brim turned up on one side (a fashionable revival of the late-eighteenth/early-nineteenth-century shape of hat). All these hats were popular forms of adult female millinery in the years between 1908 and 1912.

Body The girls all wear short, knee-length dresses but the level of the waist is high and the skirts are narrow. The little girl second from the left has on a broderie anglaise dress, stockings and shoes similar to those worn by Princess Mary in no. 24. The little boy (right) wears a two-piece suit with short trousers and a shirt with wide, turned-back collar.

Accessories The children wear either flat pumps or short boots.

28 Edie McNeill, 1911
H. Lamb

Note An example of a type of 'artistic' dress worn by a minority of unconventional young women in the early decades of the century. It is particularly associated with Dorelia John, wife of the painter Augustus John and sister of Edie McNeill, the subject of this portrait.

Head Her hair, in defiance of the prevailing fashion, is dressed close to the head, flat on the crown and at the sides.

Body She wears a long, loose-fitting dress with plain round neck, long straight sleeves and a dropped waistline, fastening at the centre front with a row of small buttons. It is clearly worn without a corset and rejects the idea of distorting the natural lines of the female figure (in continuation of the later-nineteenth-century principle of Aesthetic dress). Dresses of this kind were usually made of plain fabric in natural dyes giving them a suitably homespun look.

Accessories Her small hoop earrings were a familiar accessory to this type of dress and reflect a general interest among its wearers in the Romany culture.

29 Bank Holiday, 1912
W. Strang

Note A young, lower-middle-class couple are shown taking a meal out on a public holiday. They are both neatly and respectably dressed but their clothes are neither highly fashionable nor expensively tailored (as can be seen in the cut of the man's suit).

Head The young woman wears a deep-crowned velvet hat under which her hair is brushed low over her forehead and ears. The young man's hair is very short beneath his bowler hat with ribbon-bound brim and he is clean shaven. The bowler was usual with a lounge suit but it was also commonly worn by the less well-off at this time as a best hat (rather than the formal top hat).

Body Her light pink dress has a small, turned-down collar and a black belt set higher than the natural level of the waist (but not as high as on the most fashionable dresses at this date). He wears a brown lounge suit with a black spotted bow tie and a low, turned-down shirt collar. The waiter is dressed in a black tail coat, black waistcoat and bow tie; he carries a white napkin, a traditional accessory which can be traced back to the medieval period. The black suit with tail coat (for both day and evening wear) had become usual for waiters by the last quarter of the nineteenth century.

Accessories She wears long white gloves.

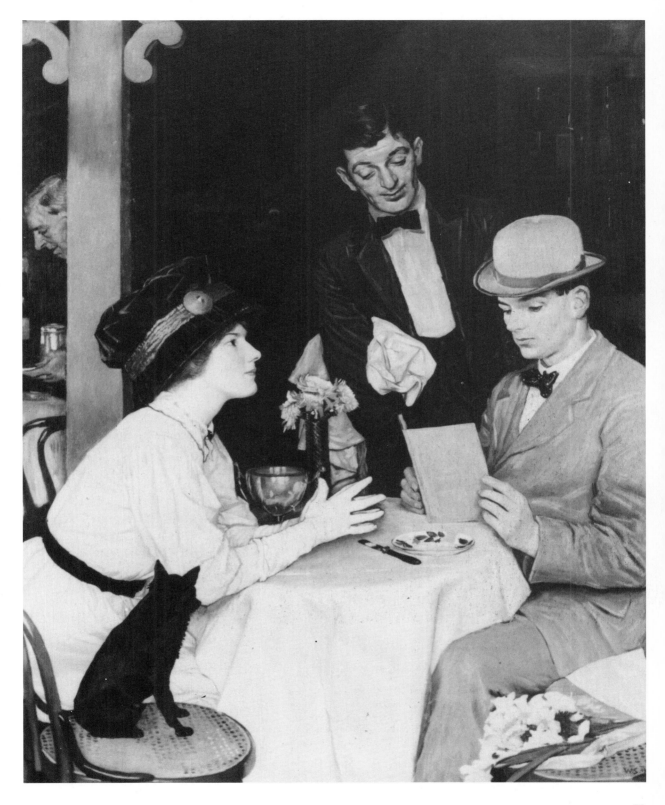

30 *Dioné – dessin de Bakst réalisé par Paquin*, 1912
L. Bakst

Note The visits of the *Ballets Russes* to Paris in 1909 and to London in 1911 made an extraordinary impact on Western Europe. In particular, the striking costumes and sets by Léon Bakst (1866–1924) with their exotic and brilliantly coloured images inspired dress designers with fresh ideas. The French couture houses of Worth and Paquin also used designs by Bakst from 1912 to 1915, openly acknowledging the debt to the Russian Ballets. Many of these designs appear to be more theatrical than conventionally fashionable but they introduced new elements which were to be absorbed into contemporary dress in the next few years.

Head The head appears small and neat with the hair dressed close to the head.

Body The general effect of this costume is fanciful and exotic with classical overtones, but it reflects the shape of the currently fashionable silhouette: long, slim and column-like. However the severe line of the *Directoire* revival is softened and blurred here by the layers of garments, tunic effects and surface decoration.

31 Dress and Undress, 1913
A. W. Mills

Note The caption to this *Punch* cartoon reads: *First Guest*. 'That Mrs Asterisk's a pretty woman, and she ain't badly got up; but she looks all wrong somehow.' *Second Guest*. 'Of course she does. The ridiculous woman persists in wearing her backbone, and backbones are quite gone out.' Women had begun to discard tightly laced corsets several years earlier and by 1913 the S-bend shape of figure induced by these was quite out of keeping with the fashionable line of dress. It is as if women, having abandoned tight lacing, now droop and sag.

Head The men wear top hats. The women's hats have deep crowns but they are generally a little smaller.

Body Formal morning suits are worn by the men. The women's dresses are long and narrow; the waistline remains high and the hobble skirt is still fashionable although the first moves towards shortening it are detectable in 1913.

Accessories Almost all the women carry parasols and the men walking sticks.

32 Along the Shore, 1914
J. Southall

See colour plate, between pp. 120 and 121.

33 Statesmen of World War I 1914–18
J. Guthrie

Note This group portrait, painted after the end of
the Great War, includes soldiers and statesmen
from India, South Africa, Canada, Australia and
New Zealand; among the seated figures are Lloyd
George and Winston Churchill.

Head Most of the men wear their hair short,
parted at the side. Over half have moustaches
including Kitchener (far right, standing) whose
face and 'walrus' moustache on recruiting posters
became one of the most popular images of the
First World War. One or two still wear the full
beard.

Body The men in civilian dress are mostly
dressed in three-piece lounge suits, the waistcoats
buttoning fairly high. The stiff, wing collar and
bow tie are worn with many of these suits. Balfour
(standing, centre right) wears a dark frock coat and
cravat. Once war broke out, fashion for men had
come to a standstill and there were no significant
developments until peace was re-established.

Accessories The man on the far left (seated)
wears spats on his feet. These had become
fashionable in the later nineteenth century and
were still seen in the first two decades of the
twentieth century though by the date of this
picture they were less common.

34 Costume by Liberty, 1916
Anon. engraving

Note In 1915 and 1916 a rather different style of dress was fashionable for women, effectively marking the end of the *Directoire* revival (although the waistline remained on the high side for several more years). The narrow hobble skirt was now abandoned in favour of a shorter, fuller one which flared towards the hem, and the waistline, though high, began to drop. This rejection of the tubular line revived some of the features of early-Victorian dress and what was considered to be a more 'feminine' silhouette (with narrow waist and billowing skirts). Shorter, wider skirts also had the practical advantage of allowing considerably more freedom of movement.

Head Her hat still has the deep, round crown fashionable before the War but it is more restrained than the millinery of the earlier period.

Body She wears a summer suit tailored in silk. The loosely belted jacket is very long and gives the fashionable effect of a tunic.

Accessories High-heeled, calf-length, buttoned or laced boots were often worn with the shorter, wider skirt.

35 Penzance Fair, 1916
L. Knight

Note Dame Laura Knight's vivid depiction of the bustle and excitement of
Penzance Fair includes the figures of several different social classes. On the
far left a nursemaid, respectably clad in a dark jacket, skirt and hat looks after
her young charges. There are some other well-dressed children to the centre
left of the picture but the boy is the foreground (right) is obviously poorer
with his tousled hair (no hat) and shabby-looking clothes. Two working-class
women behind him are drably dressed and wear practical aprons and
neckerchiefs. The two most stylish figures are the young women in the centre
foreground whose clothes reflect the fashionable new silhouette of 1915–16.

Head The two young women wear practical, pull-on hats with deep, rather
pointed crowns and narrow brims. The one on the left has her hair in thick
plaits.

Body The shorter (calf-length) and wider skirt now fashionable is worn by
the two girls in the centre. The one on the left is more informally and
unconventionally dressed in a blouse, cardigan and skirt. Long, knitted
jackets for women had appeared several years earlier for golf and other sports
wear.

Accessories The young woman in white holds an umbrella and wears high-
heeled court shoes.

36 Munitions Factory Worker, *c.* 1916
Anon. photograph

Note By 1916 the War showed no signs of ending and women were being called upon to help in the war effort, working in hospitals, canteens, factories, on the land or taking on men's jobs on the omnibuses and railways. Some jobs required women to wear breeches or trousers. This young woman, working in a South Wales munitions factory, poses in her uniform for a studio photograph.

Head Factory regulations obliged women to keep their long hair neatly dressed and covered with a cap.

Body Her thick wollen cloth suit consists of a long, loose-fitting jacket belted at the waist and ankle-length trousers.

Accessories She wears low-heeled, laced walking shoes and black stockings.

37 Fashions from *The Ladies' Tailor,* 1917
Anon. engraving

Note Towards the end of the War women's fashions returned to the tubular line fashionable before 1915. These suits, though evidently conservative in style with their long skirts flaring at the hem, reflect the narrower shape which reappeared in 1917.

Head The hair is neat and dressed close to the head. The hat on the left is close-fitting but given considerable height by an arrangement of stiffened ribbon; the one on the right has a shallower crown and a wide brim tilted forward but this too has a vertical line with the quill feathers which accompany the floral trimming.

Body Both women wear tailored costumes with short jackets and full, ankle-length skirts. The left-hand jacket has a high collar, fashionable during the First World War period. The right-hand jacket has tails like the masculine dress coat, a style which appeared several years earlier (see no. 26).

Accessories Gloves are worn by both women and they carry small handbags. Both wear high-heeled boots.

38 Lady with a Red Hat, 1918
W. Strang

Note A portrait of the writer and gardener, Vita Sackville-West (1892–1962).

Head Her large hat which has a deep crown and wide brim is worn low on her forehead concealing most of her hair. The majority of women still wore their hair long but a few more adventurous young women were cropping theirs short by 1918.

Body With her red hat she wears an emerald green jacket and buff-coloured skirt. The jacket is unbelted and has a fringed hem.

39 Inexpensive and Charming Frocks by Harrods, 1919
Anon. illustration

Note The dresses illustrated in this Harrods' catalogue are from left to right: 'Helen' Dainty Evening Frock; 'Weston' Restaurant Frock; 'Waldorf' Semi Evening Frock; 'Ritz' Smart Evening Frock. They are all made in silk georgette, crêpe de chine or net.

Head Hair is still worn long and pinned up at the back but can be arranged in shorter curls at the front. A bandeau, worn low on the forehead, is illustrated on the left (this was to be a very popular accessory to evening dress in the earlier 1920s).

Body With the re-establishment of the tubular silhouette fashionable dresses are straight and loose-fitting with the waistline still higher than the natural level; the hemline is well above the ankle even for evening wear. However the new line is muffled to some extent by the tunics added to either bodice or skirt.

Accessories Posies of artificial flowers are worn in the waistbands of several of the dresses. Shoes have high, shaped 'louis' heels and pointed toes finished with a decorative buckle.

40 Miss Muriel Gore wearing a Fortuny dress, 1919
O. Birley

Note Mariano Fortuny (1871–1949) was a dress and textile designer of Spanish birth who worked in Italy. He became particularly noted for his 'Delphos' dresses of very fine, pleated silk in subtle colours; these were outside the mainstream of high fashion and were often worn by women with artistic leanings but their classic nature has enabled them to be worn in fashionable circles from the early years of the century until the present day.

Head Her hair is long, brushed back from the face and knotted at the back of the head.

Body Her gown of thin, pleated silk is simple in shape with the sleeves cut in one with the bodice and fastened over the shoulder with buttons and loops. Although this is not a particularly fashionable garment it would not have looked out of place, in 1919, with the generally narrow and short-waisted evening gowns worn at that date.

Accessories She wears a long shawl or evening wrap round her shoulders, perhaps of a textile also designed by Fortuny.

41 The Beverley Arms Kitchen, 1919
F. W. Elwell

Note The artist lived near this old inn in Beverley and painted a number of pictures of the kitchens. This one illustrates the dress worn by kitchen maids at this period.

Head Both girls have long hair parted at the centre and knotted at the back of the head. The seated girl wears a white cap.

Body They wear plain, full-length dresses with moderately full skirts under long, white, bibbed aprons with cross-over ties at the back. Their sleeves have been pushed up above their elbows while working.

42 *Robes pour l'été 1920*
R. Dufy

Note This fashion plate from the French magazine *Gazette du Bon Ton* illustrates summer dresses in fabrics designed by Raoul Dufy and made by Bianchini-Férier. Boldly patterned textiles in abstract patterns were fashionable for garments at this date.

Head All the women wear hats but these vary in shape: the third from the left has a high crown and up-turned brim tilted onto the forehead; the one next to it has a shallow crown and wide brim; and second from the right is a deep-crowned cloche.

Body The most fashionable dresses in 1920 have the waistline at the natural level or just below and the hemline is relatively short (though well below the knee). Two styles of skirt can be worn, the straight and narrow or the fuller, dome shape.

Accessories Hats and parasols are still necessities for summer seaside wear.

43 The Ranee of Pudukota with her son the Prince of Pudukota, 1921
Anon. photograph

Note The Australian-born Mollie Fink married the Raja of Pudukota in 1915 and became a well-known figure in Society in the 1920s and 1930s. Cecil Beaton, a friend, both drew and photographed her for *Vogue* which described her, in 1932, as 'one of the leaders of contemporary chic'.

Head Her deep-crowned, wide-brimmed hat is worn low on her brow and obscures the upper part of her face. The little boy's hat echoes this shape but its narrow brim is turned up all round.

Body She wears a plain, cream silk crêpe de chine blouse and skirt by the French designer, Madeleine Vionnet (1876–1975). The blouse is loose and straight-fitting, worn outside a slim, pleated skirt reaching almost to the ankle. The Prince wears a short, wrap-over coat with a tie belt round the hips.

Accessories The Ranee's bar shoes have high, louis heels and pointed toes. She wears a string of pearls and a bracelet.

44 *La Caline*, 1922
Att. A. Marty

See colour plate, between pp. 120 and 121.

45 Edward, Prince of Wales, 1922
W. Orpen

Note Orpen's portrait depicts the Prince of Wales (later King Edward VIII and Duke of Windsor) as Captain of the Royal and Ancient Golf Club of St Andrews, Fife. Although the clothes he is wearing were intended for golf (tweed cap, knickerbockers and knitted sweater) they became popular for informal day wear for men in the 1920s and were a fashion particularly associated with the Prince.

Head The Prince's flat tweed cap has a full, pancake crown.

Body He is casually but stylishly dressed in a soft-collared shirt and tie with a geometrically-patterned, knitted pull-over, loose, checked tweed knickerbockers or 'plus fours', checked stockings and heavy, lace-up shoes.

46 Portrait of the artist's wife, Hazel in Rose and Grey, 1922
J. Lavery

Note Lady Lavery, the artist's second wife, was a noted beauty and Society hostess besides being a talented artist herself. There was an interest in Spanish dress in the early 1920s and certain features such as flounced skirts, shawls and large hair combs became fashionable for evening wear. Very long strings of pearls or beads were also popular and the way the sitter holds these is a characteristic gesture of this period (although the beads, in this instance, are not actually round her neck).

Head The sitter's hair is softly waved round her face and covers her ears.

Body She wears a light-pink dress with a close-fitting bodice and narrow shoulder straps, attached to a full, flounced skirt. A flounced shawl to match is draped over her shoulders and arms.

**47 Kynoch Cycles
advertisement,
c. 1923–5**
Anon. lithograph

Note This poster
illustrates the less
fashionable and more
practical form of dress
worn by many ordinary
women in the early
1920s. It also reflects a
new freedom for
women after 1914 in
both their clothes and
their activities. This
woman appears to be
cycling confidently and
alone about the
countryside.

Head She wears the
deep-crowned,
brimmed hat, similar to
the masculine Panama
which had appeared
during the First World
War period.

Body Her long, loose,
belted jacket (over a
blouse) and full, rather
long skirt had also been
fashionable for
informal wear a decade
earlier but continued to
be worn in the early
1920s.

Accessories She
wears buckled shoes
(see also no. 26).

48 Fashions by Swan & Edgar, 1924
Anon. illustration

Note Skirt lengths fluctuated during the first half of the 1920s but were generally well below the knee for daytime wear and ankle-length for formal afternoon and evening occasions.

Head The hat on the left is described as 'practical' and is of wool-embroidered straw; the hat on the right is in 'superior quality marocain'. Both are the deep-crowned 'cloche' style with a narrow brim.

Body On the left is a knitted wool jumper suit with accordion-pleated skirt, suitable for spring, summer and sports wear. The afternoon frock on the right is made in silk and wool marocain. The garments are unshaped and the waistline is dropped to the level of the hips.

Accessories The costumes are worn with high-heeled court shoes trimmed with decorative buckles; both women wear pendant earrings (which have now become fashionable with short hair) and one has a long string of coloured beads.

**49 Grafton Fashions for Gentlemen,
Autumn & Winter 1924–5**
Anon. lithograph

Note Correct but rather conservative, formal
clothes for daytime wear.

Head The models are wearing the correct hats to
accompany their suits: a black bowler with the
lounge suit (left) and top hat with the more formal
Chesterfield overcoat (right). Their hair is short
and both men wear small moustaches.

Body The three-piece lounge suit in herringbone
tweed (left) is worn with a striped shirt and
turned-down collar. The jacket is narrow-fitting
and the trousers are also narrow and slightly
tapered with turn-ups at the hem. He carries a
raincoat or overcoat in the raglan-sleeve style,
easier-fitting and less formal than the Chesterfield
overcoat on the right with its velvet collar and set-
in sleeve. This is probably worn over a frockcoat
or morning coat which were teamed with striped
trousers, and stiff, wing collar; this form of dress
was by now very formal.

Accessories Both men wear white handkerchiefs
in the breast pocket, gloves and white spats, and
carry a walking stick or tightly rolled umbrella.
Spats were old-fashioned by this date.

50 The Marchioness of Carisbrooke, 1925
G. Philpot

Note A Society portrait of a lady in formal evening dress.

Head Her hair is short, parted at one side and softly waved over her forehead and ears. The very fashionable 'shingle' cut of the mid-1920s shaped the hair into the nape of the neck while at the sides it was cut to the level of the ears.

Body Her full-length velvet evening dress is sleeveless and plain apart from a low and elaborately draped neckline with a jewelled ornament on the right-hand side.

Accessories A fur stole is draped over one shoulder and her long white evening gloves are clearly visible. She wears pendant earrings, a stranded pearl bracelet and a ring on her right hand.

51 Portrait of a Youth, 1925
G. Spencer

Note There is a timeless quality about this image of a working-class youth which could date from almost any time during the first 50 years of this century. The traditional working-man's dress of a cloth cap, striped muffler and easy-fitting jacket sets him apart from the mainstream of fashion.

Head The young man's short hair is just visible beneath his cloth cap and he is clean shaven. The soft cloth peaked cap was usual wear for working men by the beginning of the twentieth century and it acquired further social and political significance when it was adopted as a badge of identity by the Labour MP Keir Hardie.

Body He wears a matching jacket and waistcoat with trousers of a different cloth; he has no shirt collar or tie but their absence is disguised by the striped scarf tied round his neck. Until collar-attached shirts became common wear from the 1930s onwards, working men tended not to wear collars or ties but donned a neckcloth or 'sweat rag' to absorb perspiration when at work. This nineteenth-century practice set a precedent for wearing the scarf on other occasions in the present century – a custom which has lingered on to the present day in the form of the scarves worn by football supporters. Spencer's youth's clothes do not appear to be well-fitting and were possibly acquired second-hand.

52 A Voyage to India, 1925
H. Willebeek Le Mair

Note An illustration from a book of short stories for children by A. A. Milne. The little girl's figure has been reduced to almost a geometrical motif within the larger pattern created by the dominant vertical and horizontal lines of the window frame. This reflects the pronounced taste for linear patterns in both fashion and the decorative arts by the mid-1920s.

Head Her hair is short and straight.

Body The dress, like adult female fashions, is unshaped with a dropped waistline and ends just below the knee. The sleeves and skirt are geometrically patterned.

Accessories She wears knee-length socks and shoes.

53 The Ranee of Pudukota in a Chanel suit, 1926
Anon. photograph

Note The caption describes the Ranee as wearing 'a famous Chanel suit' and it is typical of the work of the French designer Gabrielle (Coco) Chanel (1883–1971) in the 1920s. Chanel was one of the first to introduce casual, comfortable but very elegant clothes for women in the post-war period. Her jumper suits were often made in soft, pliable, jersey-weave materials in neutral colours.

Head The Ranee's felt cloche hat is pulled well down and fits her head snugly.

Body Her three-piece jumper suit has a checked cardigan jacket and pleated skirt with a long jumper, scarf and a belt to match. The hemline is noticeably shorter (having risen in 1925 to just below the knee).

Accessories Her leather shoes have two buckled straps over the instep.

54 Advertisement by Worth, 1927
J. J. Leclerc

Note Appearing in February 1927 this advertisement illustrates clothes for visitors to the fashionable winter resorts in the South of France. The mild weather there accounts for the combination of furs and woollen scarves with short sleeves and sunshades. The hemline was at its shortest by 1927 and the fashionable silhouette taken to its slimmest extreme; however, a change in direction can just be detected now as the skirt is flared or cut with extra fullness at the hem.

Head The models wear deep felt cloches which completely conceal the hair.

Body Their dresses are short and narrow in line, with unshaped bodices and long waists. The linear emphasis is further stressed by the striped and chevron patterning of their garments.

Accessories Both women are draped about the neck and shoulders with furs (left) and a long woollen scarf (right). The fashionable parasol has a striped cover and short, rather thick handle. The woman on the left wears several bracelets on each wrist – a typical fashion of the 1920s.

55 Alfred Duff Cooper, 1st Viscount Norwich with his wife, Diana, 1927
D. Low

Note Duff Cooper and his wife were well-known figures in London Society during the 1920s, '30s and '40s. Lady Diana Cooper (born 1892) is generally considered to have been one of the most beautiful Englishwomen of the twentieth century.

Head Duff Cooper's hair is short and neatly trimmed and he wears a small moustache. Lady Diana's short hair curls out at the sides beneath her close-fitting cloche hat with a narrow brim.

Body Lady Diana Cooper wears a knee-length coat over a dress with dropped waistline and pleated skirt. Her husband is in a dark lounge suit with soft-collared shirt and knotted tie.

Accessories She carries a clutch handbag and wears high-heeled bar shoes.

56 The Botanists, 1928
J. Southall

Head The late-1920s cloche hat becomes severer in shape and more helmet-like as the brim disappears.

Body The complete lack of shaping in the fashionable dress is indicated by the loose folds round both women's waists as they sit and kneel. The skirt just covers the knees.

Accessories The woman on the left wears low-heeled bar shoes suitable for the country walking suggested by the artist.

57 Nieces of the Artist (Gabrielle and Rosemary), 1928
G. Philpot

Note The two girls are shown in their underwear, possibly getting ready for bed.

Head Their hair is cut in the shortest and severest of styles, fashionable in the late 1920s, brushed back from the face and smoothed flat over the crown.

Body Both wear loose-fitting petticoats or slips, literally tube-shaped with narrow shoulder straps. Neither appears to be wearing a brassière (which at this date was intended to flatten rather than support the bust).

Accessories Two short bead necklaces are illustrated (one on the table) and a bangle worn round the upper arm (left) – a fashion of the 1920s.

58 Evening dress by Paquin, *c*. 1928
Anon. illustration

Note In the last two years of the decade dress
designers anticipated a reaction against the stark
and functional line and tentatively introduced
both a longer hemline and gentler shaping over the
bust and hips. Eyes were gradually accustomed to
a new length by an uneven hemline – in this
instance with a skirt longer at the back than the
front. The sketch of the rear view of the dress
clearly indicates a closer-fitting skirt round the hips.

Head The hair is cut short and shaped to the
head in flat, neat waves.

Body The evening dress has a loose, chemise-
shaped bodice with the waistband at hip level and
a knee-length skirt overlaid with a longer, filmy
overskirt which dips to the ankle at the centre back.

Accessories Her only jewellery is a pair of drop
earrings; she holds a small evening bag and wears
court shoes with louis heels.

59 Mrs Jack Scudamore, 1929
D. Wilding

Note Her evening dress and coat are by the
French designer Jean Patou (1887–1936). This
photograph is much nearer in spirit to the 1930s
than the 1920s but by 1929 high fashion had
clearly adopted a softer, more sinuous line which
was achieved to a large extent by cutting and
draping fabric on the cross-grain.

Head Although the hair is still flat and neatly
waved in the style of the late 1920s the shape of the
head is becoming a little rounder and softer, and
hair begins to be grown longer over the ears and at
the back.

Body Full-length evening dresses returned to
fashion at the end of the decade; this one, in white
crêpe satin, has a draped bodice and wrapped skirt
with uneven hemline which blur and soften the
tubular shape, creating a diagonal rather than
vertical emphasis. The matching coat has a huge

Note In 1925 much wider trousers became fashionable for men and were counterbalanced by broader-shouldered jackets; these and a neat fit round the waist made the hips appear slim.

Head Hair is still worn short but can be swept back and kept in place with brilliantine. Small 'toothbrush' moustaches are the only form of facial fair favoured by young men.

Body The usual forms of evening dress are illustrated here: on the left, the less formal dinner jacket worn with a black bow tie. The single-breasted jacket is cut with wide, silk-faced lapels; the shirt has a starched front and stiff, wing collar. On the right is the formal dress suit with tail coat, white waistcoat and white bow tie. Both pairs of evening trousers have silk braid along the outer leg seams.

Accessories On the far left are the outdoor accessories to evening dress: Chesterfield overcoat, top hat, white silk scarf, gloves and cane.

shawl collar and cuffs of white fox fur, a very popular trimming during the 1920s and 1930s.

Accessories She wears pearl stud earrings and four strings of pearls. Her evening shoes are of plain white satin.

61 The Chess Players, 1929
J. Lavery

Note The sitters are the Hon. Margaret and Hon. Rosemary Scott-Ellis, daughters of the 8th Baron Howard de Walden.

Head The girl on the left has a short bob parted on one side while her sister's is cut with a fringe (a style worn by many young girls in the 1920s).

Body Both girls wear short dresses, the one on the left with the fashionable dropped waist and flounced skirt.

Accessories The sisters are still young enough to be wearing socks rather than stockings. The girl on the right has on a wrist watch.

62 Your Autumn Outfit Complete, 1930
Rex

Note Day clothes and accessories selected by the Fashion Editor, Mrs Delahaye, for *Woman's Journal*.

Head The women's heads look neat and streamlined with their small and very close-fitting hats. The fashionable 'Dutch cap' shape of the hats can also be seen on the stands.

Body By 1930 the daytime length for dresses is mid-calf and the fashionable silhouette is long and narrow. A diagonal emphasis is indicated by the use of top stitching and the wrap-over style of coat with deep shawl collar. Clothes fit closer to the figure, accentuating the slimness of the hips.

Accessories A range of accessories can be seen in the cases behind and include gloves, bags, shoes, stockings and umbrella.

YOUR AUTUMN OUTFIT COMPLETE

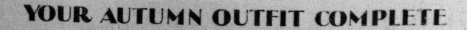

In which Mrs. Delahaye excels herself in her powers of selection. She chooses from a London store one coat and two dresses to be worn under it, with accessories which have the very best accent!

The coat is of plain brown cloth with an important roll collar and cuffs of Caracul. It has a bolero back which reflects the bolero on the afternoon dress of crêpe silk.

In the show case is the "runabout" frock in Meyer lace tweed. With the first dress you can wear the small felt of dark brown with the little feather posies over the forehead, court shoes of glacé kid stitched in beige. "La Joie" silk stockings, beige washable suède gloves, and a triangular pearl clip.

For the morning frock she selects a "cap" in brown and beige "astrakhan wool," a shoe of dark brown crocodile, and an "umbrella bag" of crocodile. The gloves are washable "Welcraft," and the stockings of artificial silk and cotton in brown and beige. All from Peter Jones (London).

Further particulars will be supplied if you write to Elsa Shelley, c/o Woman's Journal, The Fleetway House, London, E.C.4

63 G. K. Chesterton, Maurice Baring (standing) and Hilaire Belloc, 1932
J. Gunn

Note A triple portrait of the three famous writers, in day dress.

Head Two of the men wear moustaches.

Body Maurice Baring (standing) is the most informally dressed of the three in a dark, two-piece lounge suit worn over a V-necked sweater, soft-collared shirt and tie. Hilaire Belloc (right) has on a dark, three-piece lounge suit with a stiff, wing collar. G. K. Chesterton wears a long and voluminous Inverness caped overcoat over a dark jacket, waistcoat and striped trousers.

Accessories Both G. K. Chesterton and Maurice Baring are using monocles.

64 Girl Reading, 1932
H. Knight

Note This painting captures the languid mood of the early 1930s when women's fashions presented a softly-draped and fluid line.

Head The sitter's hair is worn longer than was usual in the 1920s and it is gently waved, though dressed close to the head.

Body She wears a long-sleeved blouse or jumper with a draped, cowl neck and a straight-fitting skirt.

65 Painted in a Welsh village, 1933
A. Houthuesen

Note The portrait is of a young Welshman, Harry Jones. His clothes, though respectable, are ill-fitting and were probably bought second-hand, still a common practice amongst the less well-off.

Head The brim of his felt trilby is turned up at one side in an almost stylish way but the tall crown and wide brim (which constituted a popular form of the trilby in the 1920s) are no longer fashionable and his hair is a little long and untidy.

Body He wears a three-piece lounge suit which is evidently too large and does not fit over the shoulders. His shirt has a soft, turned-down collar and his striped tie has been carelessly knotted, giving him a dishevelled air.

**66 Miss Shelagh
Morrison Bell, 1933**
J. Lavery

Note Lavery's portrait
reflects the poised, neat
and elegant character
of women's fashion in
the early 1930s.

Head Her hair is
short, parted on one
side and waved close to
her head.

Body She wears a full-
length evening dress
with low cut neckline
and narrow shoulder
straps. The skirt is cut
with fullness fanning
out from the hips. A
thin silk or chiffon
shoulder cape trimmed
with dark fur is loosely
knotted round her neck
and slips over one
shoulder.

Accessories Her
jewellery consists of
large pendant earrings
and a bracelet of dark
stones.

SHOWING UNERRING APPRECIATION OF STATUESQUE LINES AND COLOUR HARMONIES

FROCKS OF EXTREME SIMPLICITY CARRIED OUT IN UNUSUALLY INTERESTING FABRICS.

67 The Duchess of Kent as a Leader of Fashion: Dresses in Her Royal Highness's Trousseau, 1934
V. E. Norris (after Molyneux)

Note This double-page feature in the *Illustrated London News* followed the marriage of the Greek Princess Marina to the Duke of Kent. The Duchess, an acknowledged beauty, was one of the most elegant women of her generation. She was dressed by Molyneux (1891–1974), a British designer who had his couture house in Paris.

Head Her hair is short but dressed close to the head in neat waves. The hats are small and tilted forwards to one side.

Body The evening dresses on the left are slim-fitting and cut on the cross-grain of the fabric to achieve their fluid line. All three are sashed or belted at the waist. The day clothes on the right also show the pencil-thin line and longer hemline of the early and mid-1930s. The popularity of fox-fur trimming is evident but the general effect is neat and uncluttered.

Accessories Great care was taken with accessories at this date and jewellery, hats, gloves, belts, bags and shoes were carefully designed and chosen to complement the clothes.

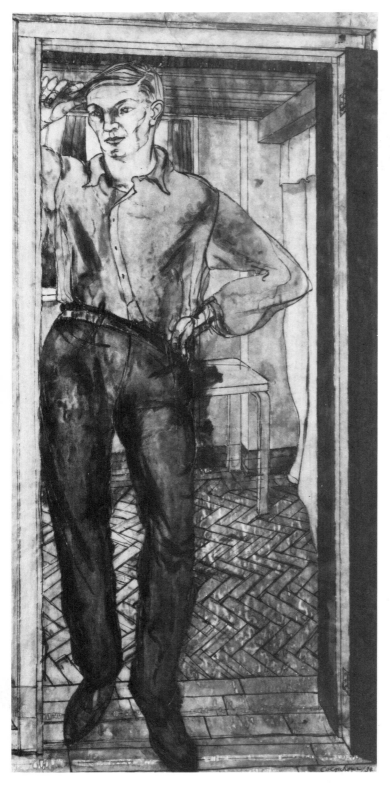

68 Humfry G. G. Payne, 1934
I. Colquhoun

Note There was a general trend towards greater informality in men's dress during the inter-war period which is reflected in this portrait of the distinguished young archaeologist, Humfry Payne, in casual clothes.

Head His hair is short and he is clean shaven.

Body He wears an open-necked shirt and medium-width trousers with waist belt and turn-ups at the hem. According to the *Dictionary of National Biography* Payne was six feet five inches tall which may account for the longer and narrower appearance of his legs than most illustrations of trousers in the 1930s.

69 Men's overcoats by Jaeger, *c.* **1934**
Anon. illustration

Note The fashion artist has caught the stylish manner in which clothes were worn in the 1930s (by both men and women). Hats were often tipped at a slight angle and coat collars turned up.

Head It is still usual for men to wear hats out of doors on almost all occasions although the top hat is rarely seen now. The style of hat depended on the formality of the suit or coat and three types are illustrated here: the formal bowler, less formal snap-brim felt hat (or trilby) and the casual flat tweed cap.

Body The two most conventional styles of men's overcoats were the fitted coat with set-in sleeves (top left) or the looser-cut coat with raglan sleeves (bottom left). In the 1930s a fashionable variation was the double-breasted overcoat with buckled belt (bottom centre). All the coats here are fashionably cut with wide shoulders; the long, lean line emphasizing narrow hips is similar to the ideal silhouette for women at this date.

Accessories The man on the left has a patterned scarf tucked into the neck of his coat. All wear gauntlet gloves.

14

70 Portrait of a Young Woman, 1935
M. Frampton

See colour plate, between pp. 120 and 121.

71 Wedding guests, 1935
Anon. photograph

Note The dress and hat worn by the lady (the mother of the bride) were designed by the British couturier, Norman Hartnell (1901–1979). Long dresses were still worn for formal afternoon functions such as garden parties and weddings. In the background the usual length for day dresses (almost mid-calf) can be seen.

Head She wears a broad-brimmed, shallow-crowned 'picture' hat in dark blue velvet. The onlookers also wear hats.

Body Her dress is of light blue silk crêpe with vertical bands of openwork embroidery; the skirt is split at the centre front to reveal a matching silk underslip. The men are in morning suits and carry top hats and gloves.

73 Mrs Ernest Simpson, 1936
The Daily Herald

Note A photograph of Mrs Ernest Simpson (later Duchess of Windsor) at Cannes in December 1936 just after the announcement of her engagement to King Edward VIII. Left to right: Lord Brownlow (Lord in Waiting to the King), Mrs Herman Rogers, Mrs Simpson and Mr Herman Rogers. The American-born Wallis Simpson though not considered conventionally beautiful was noted for her stylish good looks, slim figure and elegant clothes.

Head Mrs Simpson's dark hair is arranged in her habitual style, dressed close to the head from a centre parting.

Body Both Mrs Simpson and her friend Mrs Rogers are wearing neat, tailored cloth suits. The jacket of Lord Brownlow's double-breasted lounge suit has been hastily buttoned and hangs rather badly. The American Mr Rogers' single-breasted lounge suit is narrower in line and his shirt collar is smaller and lower than Lord Brownlow's. Both men have turn-ups on their trousers.

Accessories Mrs Simpson has a light scarf knotted round her neck and her laced shoes are cut with high vamps. Mrs Rogers wears lower-cut court shoes.

72 Day dress by Worth, 1936
Anon. illustration

Head This appears small and very neat.

Body The dress is cut in the prevailing long, narrow line. It has a high, curved neckband and padded shoulders; it is trimly belted at the waist and fits closely over the hips. Subtle decoration has been added with the horizontal and vertical pin-tucks on the sleeves and bodice.

Accessories Her matching earrings and brooch in the popular 'sun ray' motif are typical of the mid-1930s taste in jewellery and would probably have been made of clear paste stones.

74 Hiking, 1936
J. W. Tucker

Note Many sports and outdoor activities were popular in the 1930s but walking or 'hiking' was a particularly fashionable pastime for men and women.

Head All three girls wear berets although the light-coloured cap on the right is barely visible amongst the wearer's long blonde curls. Hair is neatly arranged.

Body Their hiking dress consists of short-sleeved, open-necked blouses and shorts.

Accessories They wear short socks and laced or strapped walking shoes and they carry rucksacks.

75 Mrs Gerard Simpson, 1937
G. Philpot

Head Her short hair is parted on one side, smoothed flat over the crown and curled out over the ears and into the nape of the neck.

Body She wears a plain, black evening dress and a hip-length jacket of grey silk which wraps over at the front with a long roll collar. The sleeves are full and gathered at the shoulder, tapering to the wrist in the leg-of-mutton shape (a revival of the 1890s fashion).

Accessories A wedding ring is her only visible jewellery.

72

76 Sam's wife, *c.* 1937–8
H. Holt

Note After 1933 the shoulder line was emphasized and enlarged.

Head Her hair is curled over her ears beneath a small, brimmed hat worn to one side of the head.

Body She wears a dark, collared cape fastening with square clasps, over a dark, long-sleeved dress and light neck scarf. Eastern European or peasant style embroidery was fashionable in the later 1930s.

77 Men's evening suits by Simpsons (Piccadilly) Ltd, 1938
Hof

Note The two forms of evening dress (dinner jacket and black tie or white tie and tail coat) continued to be worn. By the later 1930s shoulders were very square and padded, jackets tended to be double-breasted and boxy in shape and trousers were wide in the leg, being pleated at the front waist.

Head The hair is short but not layered, combed back from the brow and kept in place with cream.

Body The man on the left wears a double-breasted dinner jacket with very wide lapels; the dress coat on the right also has wide lapels and the fashionably square cut. Stiff, wing collars were still worn with white bow ties but a soft-collared shirt is now acceptable with a black tie.

Accessories The black bow tie is small and narrow.

SCHIAPARELLI

78 Women's suits by Schiaparelli, 1938
Anon. illustration

Note Elsa Schiaparelli (1890–1973) was the third great name in French fashion design after Chanel and Vionnet during the inter-war period. She was an Italian by birth but worked in Paris and achieved a reputation for stylish and elegant clothes which could also be amusing and unconventional.

Head Hair is now longer and loosely curled into the nape of the neck. Hats take on a more masculine, even military aspect and are higher in the crown (first and second left). A flat 'coolie' style hat is also shown (right).

Body As Europe moves towards the onset of war women's clothes appear to toughen up in anticipation. Tailored suits with padded shoulders and shorter skirts are worn although a feminine appearance is preserved with the emphasis on a narrow waist.

Accessories The rather severe line is lightened by the decorative buttons (Schiaparelli was particularly noted for her choice of original buttons), the pair of cupid clips in the lapels (left) and the fox fur scarf (centre). All three women wear gauntlet gloves.

79 Street Scene, 1939
B. Freedman

Note This impression of a busy urban street illustrates the range of clothes that might be seen at this time – from the well-dressed ladies, street musician and scruffy boys in the foreground, to the respectable passers-by and traders in the background.

Head Almost every adult is wearing a hat or cap of some kind. Most of the men are shown in soft felt trilby hats (including the street musician) or cloth caps but there is still an old-fashioned gentleman (to the left in the background) who is wearing a top hat with either a frockcoat or Chesterfield overcoat. Although the women all have their heads covered, mostly with small neat hats tilted at an angle, the younger girls and children are bare-headed, hinting at the eventual decline of hat-wearing in post-war years. Young girls are also wearing their hair longer than in the earlier 1930s; the girl on the extreme right has a hair-band tied in a bow, a style which was to continue to be popular in the 1940s.

Body The two women in the centre foreground wear fitted coats with large collars; the shoulders are only moderately padded and the line of the skirt is still fairly long and narrow in the style of the mid 1930s. The young girl behind is more casually dressed in blouse, skirt and long jacket. The two boys in the foreground, though they are wearing suits and one carries a cap, give the appearance of shabbiness with their badly fitting and crumpled clothes. The boy on the left has no tie, his trousers are too short and his socks are falling round his ankles.

Accessories The women's handbags are still small and rectangular, often held under the arm. Their shoes have long, narrow toes and there is an example of the T-bar fastening fashionable for women's shoes in the 1920s and 1930s.

80 Afternoon gowns by Debenham and Freebody, 1939
Anon. illustration

Head The women on the left and right wear their hair swept up and curled at the front. The hats are tall and narrow in shape, tilted to one side and gaily trimmed with ribbon bow, artificial flowers and a veil.

Body The dresses, intended for smart day wear in town are knee-length and fitted over the bust, waist and hips; the shoulders are padded and the waist tightly belted. The dress and jacket on the left are ornamented with padded scroll motifs; the two on the right are ruched across the bust.

Accessories High-heeled court shoes are worn; two of the pairs have open toes, a fashion which appeared in 1936.

81 Alexander Gavin Henderson, 2nd Lord Faringdon, 1930–40
W. Sickert

Note Painted between 1930 and 1940, this portrait shows the style of suit fashionable for men at the outset of World War II.

Head His hair is short and neatly trimmed and he is clean shaven.

Body His lounge suit has a square cut jacket hanging straight from a padded shoulder line and the trousers are very wide and long. With it he wears a soft-collared shirt and knotted tie.

Accessories He has a white handkerchief in the breast pocket.

82 Twin set and tweed skirt by Harrods, *c.* 1939–40
Anon. illustration

Note With the outbreak of war women's fashions took on a more practical aspect; nevertheless the artist has suggested the ideal silhouette with its emphasis on wide shoulders and slim waist and hips.

Head Her hair is neatly tied up in a turban-like scarf, a fashionable and informal alternative to the hat in the early 1940s.

Body She wears a knitted jumper and matching cardigan with a checked tweed skirt. The hemline is just below knee level and the skirt is given some fullness with its inverted pleats.

84 'Stand up to It', Nicolls advertisement, 1940
Anon. illustration

Accessories She has a charm bracelet round one wrist (these had become popular around 1935) and she wears sensibly heavy footwear.

83 Lady Caroline Paget, early 1940s
R. Whistler

Head Her hair is parted at the centre and lies close to the head in neat waves; but it is longer than was fashionable in the 1930s.

Body She is dressed in a light, collarless coat with padded shoulders and waist belt over a dark dress which is high to the neck.

Accessories High-heeled court shoes are just visible in this unfinished portrait.

Note War-time conditions demanded practical, comfortable and hard-wearing clothes. Indispensable items in a woman's wardrobe were an overcoat, tailored suit and day dress. An innovation was the all-in-one shelter suit (also called a siren suit) – warm and easy to put on for night-time visits to air-raid shelters.

Head The increasing masculinity of women's fashions is softened by longer and more elaborate hair styles. Hats are still considered to be necessary accessories.

Body The coat and suit jacket are cut with wide shoulders and broad lapels and present a uniform appearance. The button-through dress is tailored in a similar manner. The shelter suit (top) is a combined hooded jacket and trousers in woollen cloth.

Accessories Heavy, laced walking shoes are worn with the outdoor coat and suit while a lighter (but still sensible) court shoe is illustrated with the dress.

85 The Artist's Family, 1940–43
H. Lamb

Note The artist, Henry Lamb, with his wife, Lady Pansy Lamb, and their children, Henrietta, Felicia and Valentine at their home.

Head The artist's wife wears her hair in a long, curled bob. Both girls have their hair cut in a fringe.

Body The little girls wear short, pleated skirts and a knitted jumper or cardigan. Their mother is dressed in a blouse or jumper, cardigan jacket and straight-fitting skirt. The artist wears a light sports jacket and dark trousers.

Accessories The parents are both wearing indoor slippers while their daughters wear white socks and bar shoes.

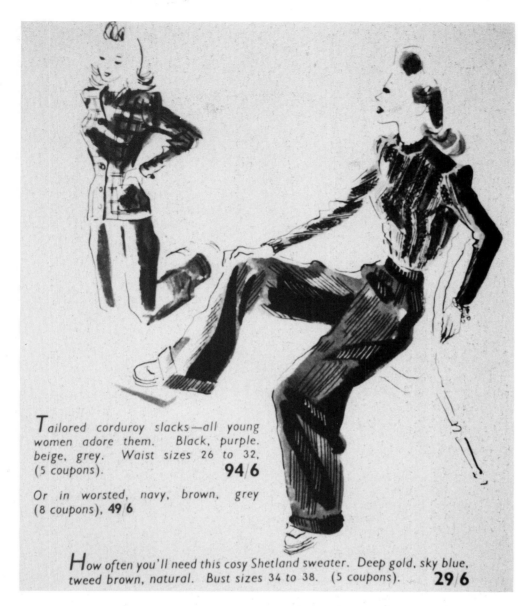

Tailored corduroy slacks—all young women adore them. Black, purple, beige, grey. Waist sizes 26 to 32. (5 coupons). **94/6**

Or in worsted, navy, brown, grey (8 coupons), **49/6**

How often you'll need this cosy Shetland sweater. Deep gold, sky blue, tweed brown, natural. Bust sizes 34 to 38. (5 coupons). **29/6**

86 Tailored corduroy slacks by Harvey Nichols, 1941
Anon. illustration

Note Trousers had been worn by some women for informal, daytime occasions (especially on the beach) since the 1920s but it was not until the late 1930s that the fashion became very widespread. Slacks proved to be particularly practical and warm during the War – the Harvey Nichols catalogue said, 'all young women adore them'.

Head The hair is shoulder-length with the front rolled back to give it height.

Body The young woman on the right wears a short, knitted Shetland wool sweater and corduroy trousers with wide legs and turned-up hems. The girl on the left has a tailored jacket with her trousers.

Accessories The right-hand model wears a lucky charm bracelet on her left wrist.

87 'Every Coupon Counts', 1942
Anon. illustration

Note The dress patterns featured in this issue of *Weldon's Ladies' Journal* are recommended for their economical use of clothing coupons. Clothes rationing was introduced in June 1941 limiting, with the use of coupons, the acquisition of clothing by all civilians. This was followed in 1942 by a series of Making of Clothes (Restrictions) Orders by the Government.

Head The hair is shoulder-length and in some cases worn with a curled fringe or rolled back from the temples. Hats (which were exempt from rationing) have tall crowns.

Body Clothes rationing and Utility regulations limited the design of women's dresses. The early 1940s saw little development apart from an intensification of the features fashionable on the outbreak of war: wide shoulders, narrow waists and short skirts. The dresses illustrated here have attempted some variety in the basic style with yokes, insets and contrasting panels. A classic 'Box Coat for all occasions, all weathers, all seasons of the year' appears on the far left.

Accessories Most of the footwear is heavy and practical. A touch of femininity is given by the bracelets worn by the seated model who also carries a large handbag.

88 Utility suit, 1942
Anon. photograph

Note A Utility suit of woollen tweed and rayon crêpe blouse both designed by the Incorporated Society of London Fashion Designers for the Board of Trade. Leading London couturiers formed themselves into an Incorporated Society in 1942 to promote the interests of the British fashion industry in the face of war-time restrictions; they worked with the Board of Trade to produce a range of well-designed and fashionable clothes for the ready-to-wear market which at the same time observed the limitations of the Utility Scheme. The results were some stylish designs, an example of which is this suit (preserved in the collections at the Victoria and Albert Museum, London).

Head The head was virtually the only area in which women were able to exercise any originality and femininity during the war period. The model here wears her hair neatly groomed beneath her smartly tilted felt hat. Make-up, especially dark red lipstick, was used (when available) and reflects the influence of American film stars such as Joan Crawford.

Body Her tailored suit has a hip-length, waisted jacket with patch pockets and four large buttons from high, wide lapels; the skirt is panelled and slightly flared, just covering the knee cap.

Accessories She wears earrings and dark gloves.

**89 Sir Ernest Gowers, Lt-Col A. J. Child and
K. A. L. Parker in the London Regional Civil
Defence Control Room, 1943**
M. Frampton

Note At a time when most men were in uniform
this portrait is unusual in its clear depiction of
civilian men's dress of the early 1940s; it shows the
style of clothing now preferred for off-duty wear
and what could also be worn in some offices (for
example, a crew-necked sweater with collar and tie
or a polo-necked jumper and sports jacket as well
as the more usual lounge suit).

Head The hair is short and very neat in the 'short
back and sides' style usually associated with the
armed services. The seated man's spectacles have
the circular, narrow-rimmed frames which were
the common style at this period.

Body Sir Ernest Gowers (left) wears a three-piece
lounge suit and is more formally dressed than the
other two men in their knitted sweaters.

90 Pauline in the Yellow Dress, 1944
J. Gunn

See colour plate, between pp. 120 and 121.

91 A Land Girl and the Bail Bull, 1945
E. Dunbar

Note The Women's Land Army was re-formed just before the outbreak of World War II and, as in 1914–18, it made an important contribution to the war effort.

Head Her hair is pinned up and her head protected by a soft, deep-brimmed hat.

Body She wears the regulation Land Army dress of shirt, green jersey, khaki breeches, woollen stockings and heavy, laced shoes under her overalls.

92 The Doublet Jacket by I. Magnin, 1945
Duran

Note A brown and white skarkskin suit with doublet jacket 'for Spring excitement' advertised by I. Magnin & Co. of California. America did not enter the war until 1942 and although not subjected to such stringent clothing restrictions as Britain, her fashions followed similar lines. The wide shoulders and short, straight skirt were also worn but American clothes managed to look both pretty and practical.

Head The essentially masculine shape of her hard straw hat is softened by the ribbon trimming and face veil.

Body The suit jacket has taken shoulder width to its extreme and gives the impression of broad epaulettes. The sleeves are cuffed and the slim-fitting jacket is neatly belted at the waist. The skirt is narrow and reaches well over the knee.

Accessories Large, round earrings and chunky jewellery at the neck and wrist have been suggested by the artist. Short, white gloves complete the outfit.

The doublet jacket

brown and white sharkskin suit for Spring excitement

Duran

I. Magnin & Co. California

93 New York by Starlight, 1946
Anon. illustration

Note A fashion illustration showing evening
dresses by leading American dress designers:
Hattie Carnegie, Adele Simpson, Nettie
Rosenstein and Muriel King. 'Skirts are as you
please', the caption reads, 'willow slim, draped or
full as a crinoline – there is agreement only in the
handspan waists and revealing necklines'. For the
first year after the War there was uncertainty
about the direction in which fashion was to move
but many designers responded to a general
yearning for greater luxury and femininity with
skirts which were nostalgically full or draped.

Head The women's hair is worn long and swept
up over the crown for evening.

Body These dinner and dance dresses have low-
cut necklines with shoulder straps and tight-fitting
bodices making the waist appear as small as
possible. All the fabrics are boldly patterned and
some are trimmed with ribbon rosettes or artificial
flowers.

Accessories On the far right is illustrated a black
net boa, described as 'very Edwardian'. Cluster
earrings and choker necklaces are fashionable.

Hattie Carnegie   Adele Simpson   Nettie Rosenstein   Muriel King

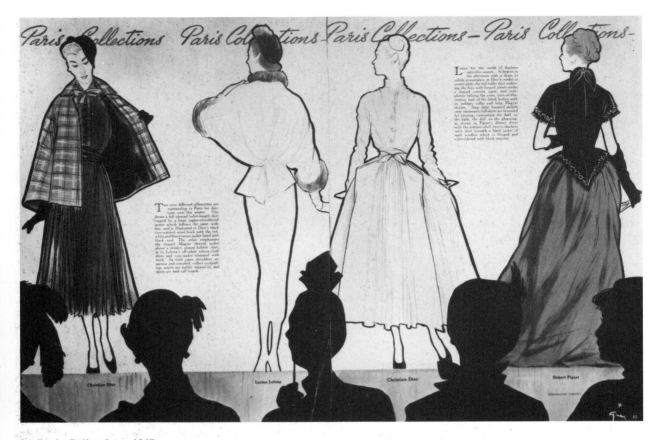

94 Paris Collections, 1947
R. Gruau

Note Dresses by Christian Dior (1905–57), Lucien Lelong and Robert Piguet reported in a November issue of *Woman's Journal*. Christian Dior's first collection, introducing the 'New Look' in the Spring of 1947, brought him instant fame; he followed it up with a second New Look collection in the autumn and he was quickly copied by other designers and manufacturers. The New Look consisted of much longer, fuller skirts for day wear, tiny waists, softly-shaped bodices with a rounded shoulderline and many decorative details. It embodied most of the features which had been lacking in war-time fashions: colour, luxury, prettiness and femininity.

Head The hair, though long, is neatly arranged and worn closer to the head beneath small, trim hats.

Body Dior's dresses (first and third from left) have small standing collars, narrow and rounded shoulders, tightly belted waists and full, pleated, calf-length skirts. There was an alternative New Look silhouette (illustrated second left in a suit by Lucien Lelong) which had a long, narrow skirt.

**95 Queen Mary inspecting the latest 'New Look' tweeds at the
International Wool Secretariat showrooms, London, 1948**
A. Goodchild

Note The New Look was greeted with enthusiasm by most women in Britain
although many officials disapproved. Clothes rationing was still in force and
made the new styles seem extravagant and expensive. However,
manufacturers were able to produce an approximation of the line within
reasonable prices. This model by the London couturier, Mattli, has far less
material in the skirt than Dior would have used. Ironically, Queen Mary's
skirt is fashionably long although she had not significantly altered the length
of her dresses since the hemline began to rise in 1913.

Head The model's hair is longer than that of the other women in the room
but it is tightly drawn back.

Body The tweed dress reflects the main features of the New Look – less
padding in the shoulders, a fitted waist and longer, fuller skirt. It has a three-
quarter length jacket to match. Queen Mary and her neighbour wear floral
print dresses. The light has caught the clumsy metal zip of the black dress in
the foreground.

Accessories Queen Mary wears her habitual toque and shoes which are
closer in style to the 1920s than the 1940s. The model's open-toed shoes have
thick high heels and platform soles. Her hat is small and flat in the crown.

A 3   A 11   A 10   A 12   A 2   A 8   A 1

HERE are illustrations of the full series of our styles in the Stock Block service. Readers will find these stock blocks invaluable for illustrating their local press advertisements, brochures, letterheads, etc. There are at pre-

STOCK BLOCKS

sent thirteen different styles available which we illustrate individually each week. Blocks

are available 3in. deep by approximately 1in. wide (as illustrated), and priced at 19s. 6d. Readers requiring stock blocks should apply to "Stock Blocks," Tailor and Cutter House, Gerrard Street, London, W.1.

A 13   A 5   A 7   A 6   A 9   A 4

96 'Stock Blocks'. Men's clothes by the *Tailor and Cutter*, 1948
Anon. engraving

Note The 13 figures illustrate the main styles of dress in the post-war male wardrobe: dinner jacket and dress suit for evening wear, double or single-breasted lounge suits for the daytime and several different types of overcoats.

Head Hats are still considered essential but only two styles appear here: the formal bowler and the less formal, soft felt trilby. The hair is cut short. The men are either clean shaven or have small moustaches.

Body The fashionable line is an exaggerated version of the later 1930s style of dress – the shoulders are very broad but jackets taper to fit neatly round the hips. Lapels are wide and long, dropping to a low-set, double-breasted fastening. Trousers are wide with turn-ups. All shirt collars are soft for day wear but the stiff, wing collar still appears with evening clothes.

Accessories Gloves, sticks or tightly furled umbrellas are usual. Half the men are pictured smoking cigarettes or pipes.

97 Evening dress by Worth, 1948–9
Anon. drawing

Head The model's hair is short. The long, elaborately curled hairstyles of the war period pass out of fashion at the end of the 1940s.

Body Her evening dress has a fitted, strapless bodice and long, full skirt. The strapless bodice was a new fashion which was to remain popular throughout the 1950s. It was usually boned to give it additional support.

Accessories She wears a double-stranded, choker necklace.

98 Bathing costumes and beach wear by Harvey Nichols, 1949
Anon. illustration

Note During the War many beaches (especially on the South Coast) were mined or fenced off and fashions in swimwear had been restricted by austerity regulations. After the War interest in beach clothes was revived and colourful new styles were introduced, the most notable of which was the 'bikini', a briefer version of the two-piece bathing costume (which first appeared in 1935) named after a Pacific atoll used for atom bomb tests in 1946.

Body The sun dress (left) has a strapless, boned bodice and full, calf-length skirt similar in style to fashionable evening dresses; it is worn with a matching bolero jacket in a brightly printed cotton. The button-through dress next to it has a two-piece sun or swim-suit to match. The one-piece costumes on the right are made of elasticized rayon satin and wool jersey (nylon had not yet come into use for swimwear). The beach coat is of terry towelling.

Accessories Sunglasses, rubber swimming caps and sandals with long ties criss-crossing the ankles are worn by the models.

99 T. S. Eliot, 1949
P. Wyndham Lewis

Note Although the shoulders of the jacket are broad this suit presents a trimmer, more elegant appearance than those of the mid-1940s. Loose, boxy jackets and wide trousers were passing out of fashion in favour of a narrower silhouette. The adoption of dark suits and white shirts added a certain drama and refinement and this change in the style of men's dress can be regarded as the masculine equivalent of the New Look for women – a rejection of dreary, shapeless wartime suits.

Head His hair is short but not layer-cut so that it lies flat and close to the head when swept back from the brow.

Body He wears a dark, three-piece lounge suit, white, soft-collared shirt and dark tie.

Accessories There is a white handkerchief in his breast pocket.

**100 The Teaching Staff of the Painting
School, Royal College of Art, 1949–50**
R. Moynihan

Note The sitters are from left to right: John
Minton, Colin Hayes, Carel Weight, Rodney
Burn, Robert Buhler, Charles Mahoney, Kenneth
Rowntree, Ruskin Spear and Rodrigo Moynihan.

Head Several of the younger men wear their hair
a little longer than the conventional length but in
general the hair is short and neatly groomed.

Body The artists wear either lounge suits or
sports jackets and flannel trousers (which are
moderately wide with turn-ups). After the War
waistcoats were less often worn as the more
informal two-piece suit was preferred. Almost all
the men here wear collars and ties (there is one
bow tie, second from the left).

101 Suit by Worth, 1949–50
Anon. sketch

Note This fashion illustration catches the essential elements of the ideal look at this moment: a small neat head, the traditionally feminine 'hourglass' figure and long legs whose shapeliness is both concealed and revealed by the tight-fitting skirt.

Head The artist conveys with a few lines a fashionable, tiny pill-box hat, earrings, and lips accentuated by dark lipstick.

Body The two-piece suit has a high collar open at the neck (the jacket is intended to be worn on its own, not with a blouse or jumper underneath). Shoulder width is still emphasized but the waist is very sharply indicated and the hips are rounded. The skirt is long and narrow.

Accessories She wears bracelet-length gloves.

for Ascot
A wonderful picture hat in pink crinoline, with curled ostrich feathers.
also available in navy, black or white. £9 . 9 . 0
Soft pouchy bag in grosgrain, navy or black. size 10 x 6 with 4½ in. base.
£6 . 19 . 6
Fine French suède elbow-length gloves in navy, brown, pastel pink,
grey, beige or black. £3 . 15 . 6
Elegant platform shoes in grosgrain. Navy, brown or black.
American sizes 5—8½. £5 . 9 . 6

**102 Accessories for
Ascot by Harvey
Nichols, 1950**
Anon. photograph

Note Fashion models
of the 1950s were noted
for their poised but
haughty expressions.
The emphasis was on
perfect make-up and
grooming and this
involved particular
attention being paid to
fashion accessories.

Head Her hair is
brushed back from the
face and smoothly
dressed beneath a
wide-brimmed picture
hat in pink net with
curled ostrich feathers.
The eyes, eyebrows
and lips are
accentuated with
cosmetics.

Body Her lace dress
has a low, shaped
neckline and short
sleeves.

Accessories She
wears elbow-length
suede gloves and
displays a silk grosgrain
court shoe with high
heels and platform
soles; the handbag in
matching grosgrain (a
firm, corded silk fabric)
is soft and pouchy in
shape.

103 Conversation Piece at the Royal Lodge, Windsor, 1950
J. Gunn

See colour plate, between pp. 120 and 121.

104 Family Group, 1951
E. Halliday

Note An informally posed portrait group, from left to right: Lady Harlech, Lord Salisbury, the Duchess of Devonshire and Lord David Cecil.

Head Both men have short, neatly cut hair; the women's hair is also short and neatly dressed close to the head.

Body Lord Salisbury (second left) wears a dark, three-piece lounge suit with white shirt and dark tie; his brother is less formally dressed in a light, two-piece lounge suit and bow tie. Lady Harlech and the Duchess of Devonshire wear V-necked dresses with strings of pearls.

105 Advertisement for children's clothes by Cherub, 1952
C. Wood

Head The boy's hair cut is modelled on an adult man's style. The girl's long hair is arranged in two plaits tightly pinned to the top of her head and finished with two ribbon bows.

Body Both children wear knitted garments: a plain, round-necked jumper for the girl, with a checked cloth skirt, and a short, V-necked, patterned cardigan for the boy, over a round-necked shirt and shorts.

Accessories The girl wears short, white socks and flat bar shoes.

106 Caroline, 1953
R. Jacques

Head Very short hair
giving an 'urchin' or
'gamine' look was
fashionable in the early
1950s. Eyebrows were
ideally thick and dark
and the lips full.

Body Her evening
dress has a strapless
bodice which would
have been firmly
boned. With it she
wears long evening
gloves and a bead
choker necklace. Her
bracelet is worn over
her glove.

MARSHALL &
SNELGROVE
OXFORD STREET
LONDON W·1

PURE *Silk* DRESS *perfectly tailored with a well pleated skirt. In gold, pink, pale green & peach.* Hip sizes 36, 38, 40, 42 6½ GNS.

PURE *Silk* DRESS *straight skirt, lined throughout. A lovely print in Pink/black, yellow/black, grey/black, turquoise/black.* Hip sizes 36, 38, 40, 42 10½ GNS

INEXPENSIVE GOWN SALON · First Floor

2

107 Silks in May, dresses by Marshall and Snelgrove, 1954
Anon. illustration

Head The hair is arranged in a short, feathery cut with a small fringe.

Body The two most popular styles of day dresses in the mid-1950s are illustrated here. On the left is the slim-fitting, shaped sheath – in this example with cap sleeves cut in one with the bodice and with hip pockets. On the right is the classic shirt-waister with a buttoned bodice, collar and revers, cuffed sleeves, narrow waist belt and full, pleated skirt.

Accessories The more formal outfit on the left is completed by a picture hat with round, shallow crown and wide brim, bracelet-length gloves and clutch handbag. Short, white gloves are worn by the model on the right and she holds a parasol. Both models wear large, round earrings.

97

108 From Narrow to Wide: Dior's 'A' line, 1955
Anon. illustration

Note Christian Dior was the first couturier to christen each collection with a theme name or line. Probably his most famous, after the New Look, was his 'A' line in 1955, described here as 'the uninterrupted length of bodice from narrow shoulder to banded hip, with the lightly fitted waistline. Avoidance of nearly all trimming gives that completely plain look which is this season's chic.'

Body On the left is a linen dress with full skirt, just below knee-length; next to it is a tailor-made suit in shantung silk with hip-length, fitted jacket and wide, pleated skirt. The strapless ball gown, though its skirt is full, recalls the 'Empire' line with its waistband just below the bust.

Accessories Formal hats and long gloves are worn with the day clothes. Shoes are lighter in appearance, with slimmer, high heels and pointed toes

From Narrow to Wide

*selected by Elsa Shelley
at the Paris collections*

HERE is Dior's A line with the uninterrupted length of bodice from narrow shoulder to banded hip, with the lightly fitted waistline. Avoidance of nearly all trimming gives that completely plain look which is this season's chic. You see this new silhouette in the first dress of linen with the spreading skirt, and in the suit where the line is emphasised by a finely pleated skirt. This tailormade is of the fashionable shantung which also makes Dior's guilelessly perfect Empire evening dress.

DIOR

Réproduction Interdite

F 59

109 Night into Day, men's suits by Simpsons, 1955
Hof

Note Two of the most common forms of dress for men in the 1950s: the dinner suit for formal evening wear and the lounge suit by day. The suits in this advertisement are in lightweight cloths for the summer or holidays abroad.

Body The dinner jacket (left) has retained the square shoulders, wide, silk-faced lapels and double-breasted fastening so fashionable during the 1940s and its conservative appearance tends to enhance its formal nature. However a concession to contemporary fashion has been made with the adoption of a soft-collared shirt and rather jaunty, narrow bow tie. The lounge suit (right) reveals the slimmer line and single-breasted fastening now preferred in the 1950s. The jacket is shorter and more fitted with narrower-cut trousers than those of the immediate post-war period.

Accessories The man in the lounge suit carries a light straw hat. Both men have white handkerchiefs in the breast pockets of their jackets.

110 Lady Pamela Berry, 1956
Anon. photograph

Note Lady Pamela Berry (later Lady Hartwell) became President of the Incorporated Society of London Fashion Designers in 1954.

Head Her hair is gently waved from a centre parting and rolled into the nape of the neck. She has on a small, close-fitting hat with a veil over her face.

Body She wears an easy fitting, V-necked dress with short sleeves cut in one with the bodice.

Accessories Her long gloves are dark, to match her hat and handbag; she wears a bracelet on each wrist, over the gloves, a four-strand pearl necklace, flower brooch and earrings.

111 The Pink Hat, 1956
V. Ilsley

Note An illustration from an American children's book. Although hats were worn far less by children in the 1950s they were still seen on formal occasions and were obligatory wear for British schoolgirls.

Head The mother's hair is long and knotted at the back of her head; her flat-crowned and brimmed hat is slightly tilted forward as a result. The little girl's straw hat is completely flat and ties under the chin with ribbons.

Body The woman wears a suit with a large collar and long jacket; the line is narrow but much less fitted round the waist than the earlier 1950s style. The child's dress is knee-length with a full skirt.

Accessories The woman's trim appearance is complemented by a neat clutch bag and high-heeled court shoes. The little girl wears short socks and flat shoes and she carries a small handbag.

112 Casual clothes by Jaeger, 1956
R. Gruau

Head In the later 1950s the hair is grown longer and styles become softer and fuller.

Body The model on the left wears a chunky, knitted pullover with a shawl collar, and ankle-length, tweed slacks; the girl on the right has a thick, knitted cardigan with her wrap-over, checked tweed skirt.

Accessories The trousers are worn with flat pumps, the tweed skirt with low-heeled court shoes.

113 Hugh Gaitskell, 1957
J. Cassab

Note An informal portrait of the Labour politician and Party Leader, Hugh Gaitskell (1906–63).

Head The hair is short and neat and he is clean shaven.

Body He is dressed in a green sports jacket and buff trousers with a white shirt and dark green tie. There is no exaggerated padding of the shoulders and his shirt collar is small and rather narrow.

114 Teddy Boy wedding, Lancaster, 1957
Syndication International

Note A photograph of David Hamm and his bride, Mary Crawshaw with their best man, Bobby Donaghy, and bridesmaid, David's sister Gwen at St Luke's Church, Skerton, Lancaster on 22 May 1957. The two men wore matching powder blue suits edged with black velvet. The Teddy Boy style of dress first emerged around 1952 in the East End and North London and by 1956 could be seen all over Britain before passing out of fashion after 1958. Its characteristic features were a long jacket (retaining the pronounced shoulderline and 'drape' cut of the 1940s), trousers with straight and very narrow legs (sometimes tapered to the ankle), narrow ties, yellow socks and large, crêpe-soled shoes (called 'creepers'). Fancy waistcoats could also be worn and the hair was cut with a long quiff at the front slicked back with grease. It is interesting to note that while the bridegroom and best man have opted for this unconformist style of dress for a church wedding the bride and bridesmaid in their tailored suits are quite conventionally, if not dowdily dressed for this date. The bridesmaid's skirt is unfashionably long recalling, with her padded shoulders and indented waistline, the fashions of the late 1940s.

Head The girls' hair is short and curled but covers the ears in the longer style favoured towards the end of the decade. Both wear small, close-fitting hats, the bride's with a short veil covering her face. Both men have their hair arranged in the classic Teddy Boy 'duck's arse' hair cut. It is noticeable that neither of them wears

or carries a hat (an item deliberately discarded by the Teddy Boys).

Body The bridegroom and best man's matching suits were probably specially tailored for the occasion and are a smart version of the Teddy Boy style. Powder blue was a favourite colour (with black and maroon) and velvet collars, pointing to their Edwardian origins, were often added to jackets. Their shirt collars and ties are moderately conventional (committed Teddy Boys wore much narrower 'bootlace' ties). The bride and bridesmaid wear tailored suits with fitted jackets (over collared blouses) and straight skirts well below knee level. Suits had often been worn for weddings in the 1940s when clothes rationing and post-war austerity made it impossible or uneconomical to purchase wedding gowns or bridesmaids' dresses.

Accessories Both women carry white gloves. The bride's high-heeled and open-toed shoes appear smarter and more fashionable than the bridesmaid's almost flat-heeled courts. All four wear the floral buttonholes usual for weddings since the beginning of the century (see no. 12).

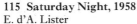

115 Saturday Night, 1958
E. d'A. Lister

Head The women have their heads covered: on the left with a scarf, in the centre with a plastic rain bonnet and on the right with a small, cap-like hat perched over the forehead. Two of the men are bare-headed (despite the rain) but the one in the centre wears one of the new style felt hats which appeared in the late 1950s, with flat-topped crown and narrow brim.

Body The clear plastic raincoats of the ladies obscure the details of their dress but they wear similar straight-fitting garments just over knee-length. The men's clothes have a sharp, tapered appearance with their coats more narrowly cut than earlier in the decade; all wear their coat collars turned up.

Accessories The women wear high, stiletto-heeled shoes with pointed toes.

116 Dress and jacket by Harry B. Popper, 1958
A. Murray

Note In the second half of the 1950s dress designers moved increasingly away from the line established by the New Look. The waistline began to wander, both above and below its normal position, and new shapes (such as cocoon-like dresses) were evolved, obliterating the natural curves of the female figure. The designer responsible for the most original ideas and who was probably the source of inspiration for this suit was the Spanish-born Cristobal Balenciaga (1895–1972).

Head The model wears a deep-crowned 'bucket' hat with down-turned brim, echoing the shape of her jacket.

Body Her checked tweed suit has a long, loose-fitting jacket ballooning out over the dress with a slim, straight skirt. This fashion demanded a characteristic stance, with the hips thrust forward to give the body a sinuous curve in keeping with the line of the clothes.

Accessories She wears white, bracelet-length gloves.

117 A Scene in Southam Street, North Kensington, 1959
C. Hall

Note A group of people in ordinary day clothes.

Head Only one woman has her head covered.

Body The women are dressed in knee-length, straight-fitting skirts with either a knitted jumper or blouse and cardigan; the little girls are similarly dressed but in fuller skirts. The men wear jackets and trousers, narrow in the leg, with turn-ups. The little boy is in shorts.

Accessories The two women on the right are wearing house slippers while the other figures have on outdoor shoes – the young women's shoes are low-heeled courts.

118 Skirts and jumpers, 1959
The Sunday Times

Head The fashion models' hair is almost shoulder-length, parted at one side and curled or 'flicked' out over the ears. By setting the hair on rollers, fuller hairstyles became possible in the late 1950s.

Body The line of the classic skirt and jumper has changed. Knitted sweaters are longer and looser fitting, worn with skirts which flare at the hem in a gentle A-line.

Accessories The shoes have a spiky look with their narrow, pointed toes and high, thin heels.

119 Concert at the Chelsea Arts Club, 1960
P. Wyeth

Note This appears to be an impromptu recital at an informal gathering. Almost all the men are casually dressed, some still in their outdoor clothes.

Head Several of the men have full beards and one has a long 'handle-bar' moustache. The beards indicate the artistic leanings of the sitters. By this date beards were rarely seen on conventional men (except for a few very elderly and old-fashioned gentlemen or naval officers) but they were grown by a small number of artists, writers and intellectuals as a badge of non-conformity.

Body The man in the centre wears a checked sports jacket over a zipped, knitted cardigan, shirt and tie. Those on either side of him are wearing knitted sweaters (in most cases over shirts and ties) but the man on the far left with the billiard cue is in shirtsleeves, fancy waistcoat and cravat. In the foreground two duffel coats and an informal, fur-collared jacket can be seen while the men at the back wear more formal overcoats in established styles.

Accessories Long scarves and hats are worn by several of the men.

120 Mrs David Muirhead, 1960
W. Dring

Head Mrs Muirhead's collar-length hair is swept back from her face in a layer-cut and softly waved style given height on the crown.

Body She wears an easy-fitting striped blouse with stepped collar and bracelet-length sleeves pushed up her arm; her dark skirt is belted at the waist.

Accessories The open neck of her blouse is filled with a single strand pearl necklace, and her wrist watch, wedding ring and engagement ring can also be seen.

121 Helen Shapiro, 1961
Anon. photograph

Note A photograph of the young pop singer, Helen Shapiro. Although she was still only a teenager, she appears quite maturely dressed in her trim, long-sleeved dress and high-heeled court shoes. At this time there was no recognizable style of dress for teenage girls who tended to copy the adult look of their mothers' clothes – the important features of which were a straight skirt, nylon stockings and high-heels (as opposed to the schoolgirl's full or pleated skirt, socks and flat shoes). However, Helen Shapiro presents a suitably up-to-date and stylish image for a pop star with her 'beehive' hair style, slim stiletto shoes and the casual effect of her roll-necked, jersey-knit dress.

Head By 1960 the longer, fuller hair style of the late 1950s was becoming stylized into the beehive shape, often combined with 'flick ups'. The exaggerated height over the crown was achieved by setting the hair on large rollers, backcombing it vigorously and holding the structure in place with liberal quantities of hair lacquer. If the shoulder-length hair was not pinned up at the back it could be carefully set on rollers to curl or flick outwards below the ears. Her make-up concentrates on darkened eyebrows and eyes emphasized by shadow, liner and mascara.

Body She wears an easy-fitting sheath dress with bracelet-length sleeves and contrasting, ribbed-knit trimming at the neck and centre front. Although her knees are revealed when she is seated the horizontal folds of her skirt suggest that it would fall below knee level when she stood up. Nevertheless, there is an increasing focus on women's legs now and she is clearly showing off her own, clad in very fine nylon stockings.

Accessories Her shoes have the narrow pointed toes (in their most extreme form called 'winklepickers') and high stiletto heels fashionable at this date. Her only jewellery is a small wrist watch with a narrow strap.

122 Evening dress by Victor Stiebel, 1962
P. Clark

Note Victor Stiebel (1907–76) was born in South Africa and opened his couture house in London in 1932; he had a distinguished clientèle until his retirement in 1963.

Head The model's hair is dressed in an up-swept style, given considerable height and volume by backcombing – although this is a moderate version of the fashionable 'beehive' shape.

Body The evening dress of pink, floral-printed silk crêpe is a narrow, fitted sheath. The bodice and skirt are plain except for a floating panel at the back from shoulder to hem. There is a feeling of classical inspiration in the pillar-like silhouette, clean lines and lack of extraneous ornament on the dress.

Accessories Her plain, satin court shoes have pointed toes.

123 Dress and hat by Mary Quant, 1963
J. French

Note Mary Quant (born 1934) opened her first shop, Bazaar, in the King's Road, Chelsea in 1955; she began designing and making clothes shortly after and started her wholesale company in 1963. She was a young designer responding to a widely felt need for smart, youthful and inexpensive clothes for other young women in Britain. Her designs were often provocative, aggressive and amusing. The dress is modelled here by Jean Shrimpton who, with Twiggy, was one of the most famous faces of the 1960s.

Head The deliberately masculine trilby style hat is made in checked tweed to match the dress and pulled down to slouch over the eyes.

Body She wears a cap-sleeved, V-necked dress in the sheath shape but with the waistband dropped to the level of the hips. Many of Mary Quant's sleeveless dresses were dual-purpose and could be worn as pinafore dresses over a blouse or sweater by day and on their own (as here) in the evening.

Accessories It is still considered necessary to complete the outfit with bracelet-length, white gloves.

124 The Beatles, *c.* 1964
Anon. photograph

Note The Beatles did for men's dress what Mary Quant did for women's in the early 1960s. They encouraged the adoption of more casual, colourful clothes which could be identified with a teenage style of dress quite unlike the clothes of their parents. Because of their immense popularity following their early hit records in 1962–3, the influence of the Beatles was considerable. Although early photographs of the Beatles now appear somewhat tame their clothes and above all their haircuts were considered unconventional at the time and shocked older generations.

Head The Beatles popularized a new hair style for young men. Not only was the hair grown longer but it completely covered the forehead and ears in a long, thick fringe which seemed quite barbaric to older men used to the established 'short back and sides' haircut neatly swept off the brow (a style which had been worn since the beginning of the century).

Body The Beatles are wearing very tight, narrow jeans (first associated with the Teddy Boys in the 1950s). Jeans were still controversial wear for the young. In 1963 a vicar had banned boys who wore jeans from his youth club, describing a jeans-wearer as a person 'whose morals are practically non-existent' (*Daily Mirror*, 5 June 1963). Two of the Beatles wear casual, loose-fitting, roll-necked sweaters rejecting the conventional shirt collar and tie still worn by Paul McCartney (centre). Two articles of dress which were popularly associated with the Beatles at this date were the short, collarless jacket (actually designed in the original by Pierre Cardin) – not illustrated here – and the elastic-sided 'Chelsea' boot (see also no. 127)

125 Executive Type, 1964
P. Blake

Note The young executive was one of the new leaders of society in the 1960s and early 1970s – the successful, thrusting, ambitious young businessman who dressed the part in a sharp, smart way.

Head His hair is cut short and shaped close to the head but it is allowed to grow a little longer at the sides.

Body He wears a three-piece lounge suit with a natural shoulder-line and relatively narrow lapels. His shirt has a fairly deep, pointed collar which buttons on to the shirt. His tie has a thick knot and straight, narrow blade.

126 Trouser suit by André Courrèges, 1964
Anon. sketch

Note Trousers were becoming increasingly
popular for women and by 1964 were acceptable
for both evening and daytime wear although it was
not until 1967 that formal trouser suits were
generally allowed in expensive restaurants and at
Ascot. The French designer André Courrèges
(born 1923) launched an influential collection of
clothes for the new 'Space Age' in 1964. These
were notable for their clean lines and simple
shapes, crisply tailored and finished.

Head The model wears one of Courrèges's
famous 'baby bonnets' tied under the chin with a
bow. The shape of these bonnets was also likened
to spacemen's helmets.

Body Courrèges's classic trouser suit is tailored in
a firm-textured white cloth with top-stitched
seams. The jacket is straight and easy-fitting over
slim, straight-legged trousers slit at the front hem.

Accessories The typical Courrèges accessories
are short white gloves and white leather boots.

127 Dinner suit by Harrods, 1964
Anon. illustration

Note The formal dress suit (white tie and tailcoat) was rarely worn by the mid-1960s but lingered on in following decades as the recognized dress for orchestral conductors and ballroom dancers. The dinner suit with black bow tie was still usual, however, for dances and dressy occasions at night and it was brought up to date by modifications to its shape and style.

Body The new dinner suit is made of crease-resistant Terylene and worsted cloth. The jacket has a very narrow, satin-faced roll collar; the trousers are straight and narrow. It is worn with a white, pleated nylon dress shirt, small bow tie and pleated satin cummerbund. The cummerbund (originally an Indian term for a waist sash) could be worn in place of the waistcoat with evening dress as early as the 1890s but became more fashionable after the Second World War when the two-piece suit gained acceptance and waistcoats were less generally worn.

Accessories His shirt cuffs are fastened with rolled gold and black onyx links. His evening shoes are of black patent leather with elastic gussets. The elastic-sided shoe was a fashionable new style for men although it was in fact a revival of an early-Victorian form of footwear. Another version, the high-heeled, elastic-sided ankle boot, was popularized by the Beatles in 1964.

128 Dress by John Bates, 1965
J. Bates

Note This summer dress by the British designer John Bates (born 1938) was a best-selling style and was chosen as the Dress of the Year 1965 for the Museum of Costume in Bath. Bates was also designing eye-catching clothes for Diana Rigg in the ITV *Avengers* series in 1965 and he was as responsible as Mary Quant for pushing up the hemline to a new height that year.

Head John Bates' sketch recommends a short, blunt hair cut by Vidal Sassoon, its geometrical shape complementing the brief, stark line of the dress. The model's eyes are heavily accentuated with black liner, mascara and false eyelashes and her lipstick is almost white.

Body The model wears a short, sleeveless, lightly fitted sheath dress of printed linen with a see-through midriff of nylon mesh.

Accessories The dress is worn with a new style of court shoe, rounder in the toe with lower, chunkier heels.

129 Suit by Mary Quant modelled by Twiggy, 1966
The Sunday Times

Note Twiggy (Lesley Hornby) made her name as a fashion model in 1966 and dominated the look of British fashion in the last years of the decade. Her slight, boyish and adolescent figure set a new standard of thinness as an ideal of beauty.

Head Her hair is cut by Vidal Sassoon in a very short, straight and boyish style. Her eyes are heavily made-up but her complexion and lips are made to look light and clear.

Body Mary Quant's moiré waistcoat and shorts are worn with a satin shirt and 'kipper' tie. Borrowed directly from the fashionable men's wardrobe at this date, it was also called after the vaguely kipper shape of its broad, pointed blade.

Accessories As the hemline rose tights replaced stockings. She wears white tights here with her shorts.

130 Sir Francis Dashwood with his wife and children, 1966
C. Harrison

Note Although the style and manner of this family group follows the traditions of English portraiture the sitters are informally posed and their clothes reflect various features of current fashion.

Head Lady Dashwood's hair is cut in a short bob with a fringe and the sides tapered over the cheekbones. Her husband's hair is short at the back and sides. Two of their daughters have shoulder-length hair held back in a band while the third has hers cut short.

Body Sir Francis Dashwood is casually dressed in a polo-necked sweater and trousers with leather belt at the waist. His wife wears a sleeveless, high-necked dress with fitted bodice and pleated skirt. Their daughters are dressed alike in short shifts with contrasting bodices and skirts. The dresses are short-waisted in a revival (in the mid-1960s) of the 'Empire' style of the early-nineteenth century and the striped skirts reflect a contemporary taste for strong contrasts of colour and geometrical patterning. The little boy is in a loose-fitting shirt and long trousers.

Accessories The girls all wear white ankle socks and black patent leather bar shoes.

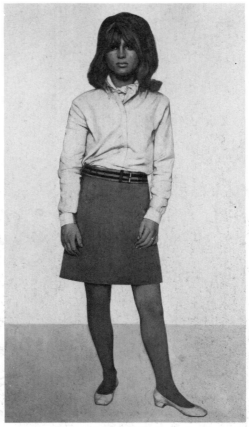

131 Dress and PVC coat by Young Jaeger, 1966
N. Eales

Note The dress, coat, hat and boots were chosen by the Fashion Editor of the *Sunday Times* as the Dress of the Year 1966 for the Museum of Costume in Bath. The clothes reflect the influence of the Paris couturiers André Courrèges and Paco Rabanne who were producing very streamlined, futuristic-looking garments in modern materials such as nylon, metal and PVC (polyvinyl chloride). Black, white and transparent fabrics were particularly fashionable in the mid-1960s.

Head The model wears a visored helmet of white leather and red PVC by Simone Mirman.

Body The dress is a brief, short-waisted, linen shift with contrasting bodice and skirt. The clear PVC coat is banded with white PVC.

Accessories The boots to match are of clear PVC and black patent leather with open toes. She is also wearing white, striped stockings originally designed by John Bates for Diana Rigg in *The Avengers* television series (first shown in 1964).

132 Julie Christie, 1967
G. de Rose

Note A portrait of the film actress Julie Christie whose looks were much admired in the middle years of the decade.

Head Her straight, shoulder-length hair has been curled and back combed to give it greater volume; her fringe is long and almost covers her eyes.

Body She is informally dressed in an open-necked shirt (with buttoned-down collar) and short, A-line skirt. The knotted scarf at her neck and wide, striped belt add to the masculine aspect fashionable for women's clothes at this date although this in no way detracts from her femininity (underlined by her long hair).

Accessories Her shoes are plain, square-toed and low-heeled pumps.

133 The Bee Gees, 1967
Polydor publicity photograph

Note During the 1960s the dress and appearance of pop singers and groups were widely emulated by the young. Many performers were close followers of fashion rather than innovators with a distinct style of their own. In this photograph the Bee Gees wear versions of currently popular fashions, albeit in rather extreme forms (as in the case of the long, skinny overcoat and flared trousers on the left and the fancy-patterned suit on the right). After 1965 more fanciful styles of dress in exaggerated shapes, lengths and colours were adopted by fashionable young men.

Head By 1967 the hair is being worn longer and fuller giving an almost girlish aspect to some men's heads. Careful cutting, shaping and even colouring of men's hair is becoming acceptable. Facial hair is returning to fashion in the form of long side burns, beards and moustaches.

Body The Bee Gees are wearing an assortment of garments but these have several features in common. Fashionable men's clothes are tighter fitting in the later 1960s, especially round the chest, waist and hips, but with more pronounced shaping – coat lapels are wider and trousers flare out at the hem in the bell-bottom shape (originally only seen in sailors' uniforms). Shirt collars are deep with long, sharp points, counterbalanced by larger ties with plump knots and wide blades. A fancy dress element in late 1960s fashion is revealed in the long, narrow, flared overcoat on the left (reminiscent of Victorian or even late-eighteenth-century men's coats) and the three-piece suit on the right. Formal suits with waistcoats are now being revived and the jacket in this example has the single-breasted fastening and sloping front edges which recall the cut of the Edwardian morning suit (see no. 1); but its loudly-patterned cloth distinguishes it from any conventional suit of the 1960s.

Accessories Jewellery is becoming fashionable for men – large rings and a chunky bracelet can be seen in this example.

134 Mini-skirts and tops by Gina Fratini, 1968
C. Benais

Note The mini-skirt was at its briefest in 1967–8. This fashion drawing illustrates the ideal image for young women: an adolescent and extremely thin figure with very long legs, a childish face and long, straight hair.

Head The eyes are made-up to look as large as possible. False lashes have been painted under the lower lids and the left-hand model also has freckles painted over her nose.

Body These brief tops, skirts and shorts for summer wear are by the British designer Gina Fratini (born 1934). Their shapes are simple and their only adornment is in the striped patterning and buckled belts.

Accessories Very large, round sunglasses became a fashionable accessory from 1965.

135 Dress by Jean Muir, 1968
Anon. photograph

Note During 1968 there was a noticeable change in the mood and direction of British fashion. In reaction against the stark, uncompromising line of the mid-1960s a new, romantic element was introduced with a longer hemline, softer shaping and more surface ornament. This is well illustrated by the choice of a dress by Jean Muir (born 1933) for the Bath Museum of Costume's Dress of the Year 1968.

Head The model's long hair is put up and elaborately arranged in loose, tumbling curls and ringlets.

Body The dress, of black-and-white spotted voile, has a high-waisted bodice and calf-length, flared skirt; the neck, bodice front, full sleeves and hem are ruffled. It was to be several years before the new, 'midi' length skirt was generally accepted but it is from this moment that the mini-skirt begins to decline in popularity.

Accessories She wears plain black patent leather pumps with square toes and low, thick heels.

136 Elizabeth Bowen, 1969
A. Durand

Note A formal portrait of an older, but elegantly dressed woman, the novelist Elizabeth Bowen.

Head Her hair is very softly waved and swept off her face into a pleat at the back.

Body She wears a full-length evening dress in the classic shape of the 1960s, the fitted, sleeveless sheath with plain, round neck (ornamented here with a tie at the shoulder). The decorative emphasis of the dress lies in its brightly patterned fabric, the oriental inspiration of which is underlined by the Chinese screen behind her.

Accessories Her jewellery includes large round earclips, a flexible bracelet and plain gold wedding ring.

7 Ena and Betty, Daughters of Asher and Mrs Wertheimer, 1901
J. S. Sargent

Note Fashionable evening dress worn by two young women in London Society.

Head Both sisters have long hair which is pinned up at the back; at the front the hair is loosely swept across the forehead in gentle waves.

Body Betty (left) wears a plain crimson velvet dress with cross-over bodice, low décolletage edged with white chiffon, and narrow shoulder straps. The waistline is emphasised and the skirt is straight-fitting, flaring towards the hem. Ena (right) wears a gown of white silk with a very low cut neckline and the shoulder seam dropped over the top of the arm; it has long sleeves extending well beyond the wrist. Her dress is looser-fitting at the waist and is cut with greater fullness in the skirt with a train at the back.

Accessories Both sisters wear ornaments of ribbon or artificial flowers in their hair and each has a jewelled clip pinned at the right hand neck edge of her dress. Betty holds an open fan in her right hand.

32 Along the Shore, 1914
J. Southall

Note The ladies are dressed for a seaside stroll although it is evident that long strides would be virtually impossible in the narrow, hobble skirts they are wearing; however the hemline has begun to rise and the dress of the woman on the right is moving towards a more practical and comfortable style.

Head By 1914 hats are smaller with narrower brims and there was a fashion for turned-up brims tilted up at the back (centre). Hair is still long and dressed with a certain amount of volume over the ears.

Body The dress on the left has the raised waistline and narrow skirt which had been in fashion for several years. The jacket and coat of the other two women suggest a lessening of emphasis on the high waist and a loosening of the silhouette while retaining its tubular line. The button fastenings are prominent on all three costumes. The little girl wears a short-waisted dress and sunbonnet.

Accessories Three different styles of footwear are illustrated: brown laced shoes (left); laced boots of black patent leather with grey cloth tops (centre) and white

bar shoes with low heels (right). The woman in the centre wears a gold wrist watch (wrist watches were beginning to replace pocket watches in the early years of the century).

44 *La Caline*, **1922**
Att. A. Marty

Note Another plate from the French magazine *Gazette du Bon Ton* (see also no. 42) illustrates a woman's dress by Doeuillet and man's jacket by Larsen.

Head The man's hair is cut very short and he is clean shaven. The woman's hair is long and drawn back over her ears.

Body The man wears a tweed sports jacket and short, tapered trousers with narrow turn-ups. His shirt has a soft, turned-down collar and his knotted tie is diagonally striped. The general effect is neat and rather sharp — the centre crease on his trousers is pronounced. The woman wears a long, loose-fitting 'tube' or 'chemise' dress with a narrow tie belt at hip level and the fabric is geometrically patterned.

Accessories The man's socks are light-coloured and he wears laced shoes. The woman's plain court shoes have moderately high heels.

70 Portrait of a Young Woman, 1935
M. Frampton

Note Meredith Frampton's portrait reflects the classical revival of the 1930s and illustrates how the fashionable, bias-cut dresses in fluid fabrics were inspired by classical draperies. As with Antique dress, the garment is intended to reveal and enhance the natural contours of the human body and in the 1930s any bulky undergarments which might destroy the line were discarded — the woman's hip bones are clearly visible through the soft clinging material.

Head The hair, though short, is long enough to cover the ears and nape of the neck; it is curled and brushed back from the forehead.

Body She wears a full-length evening dress in a light material. The bodice is cut with a deep shawl collar in a fichu-like arrangement, the gathered fabric giving the effect of drapery over the bust. The dress fits closely round the waist and hips but flares out towards the hem to fall in gentle folds — a style which is achieved by cutting the fabric on the cross-grain.

90 Pauline in the Yellow Dress, 1944
J. Gunn

Note A romantic evening dress in the 'medieval' or 'renaissance' style with its puffed sleeves and long, full skirt. The later 1930s had seen a nostalgic revival of fashions from the past.

Head Her hair is short and waved back softly but neatly from her face.

Body She wears a full-length, long-sleeved dress of a yellow patterned fabric trimmed with black velvet ribbon. The bodice has a collar and deep, V-shaped opening over a 'modesty' front, the full sleeves are banded at intervals with ribbon tied in bows. The narrow, self-material belt has a jewelled buckle.

Accessories Her jewellery consists of large pearl stud earrings and a necklace. The tip of a black, open-toed sandal can be seen.

103 Conversation Piece at the Royal Lodge, Windsor, 1950
J. Gunn

Note The Royal Family at a tea table — King George VI, Queen Elizabeth, Princess Elizabeth and Princess Margaret in day clothes. In spite of their royal status the sitters give the appearance of a fairly ordinary family — they are well-dressed without being particularly fashionable. The King and Queen are in fact quietly and conservatively dressed while Princess Elizabeth's suit still reflects the shape of the earlier 1940s. Princess Margaret, the youngest member of the family, is the most fashionable figure with her shorter hairstyle and longer, fuller skirt.

Head The Queen's hair is short and waved close to her head from a centre parting, still very much as she wore it in the late 1930s. Princess Elizabeth's is longer and more loosely waved in the shape fashionable in the 1940s but Princess Margaret's is shorter and trimmer in the new style of 1950.

Body The King, looking like most middle-class Englishmen at this date, wears a light, checked lounge suit, pale blue shirt and red spotted tie. The Queen's light blue dress is embroidered

at the neck and has bracelet-length sleeves. Princess Elizabeth is dressed in a tailored suit with pleated skirt while Princess Margaret's dress is a modified version of the New Look with a soft shoulderline, narrow waist and circular-cut, calf-length skirt.

Accessories The Queen wears red court shoes, the Princesses brown high-heeled, sling-back courts and the King brown brogued Oxford shoes.

138 Mr and Mrs Clark and Percy, 1970-1
D. Hockney

Note A portrait of the artist's friends — Celia Birtwell the textile designer, and her husband Ossie Clark, one of the chief dress designers for the fashion firm Quorum — in their Bayswater home. Mr Clark's bare feet, casual pose and challenging stare seem to be deliberately flouting the established conventions of formal portraiture as does Mrs Clark's confident pose with one hand on her hip and standing, while her husband occupies the only visible chair.

Head Mrs Clark's shoulder-length hair is arranged in loose curls framing her face. Mr Clark's hair is long enough to cover most of his forehead and ears and reaches over his collar at the back.

Body Mrs Clark wears a full-length dress, high to the neck and with long sleeves; it is softly shaped to the figure and flares at the hem. Mr Clark is informally dressed in open-necked shirt, sweater and flared, corduroy jeans.

157 Match of the Day, 1982
S. Rossberg

Note The dress of the two girls reflects the influence of the Punk movement which had emerged some six years earlier, and is thrown into sharp contrast with the sober conventionality of the clergyman's suit.

Head Each girl has dyed her hair in an intentionally obvious way (either jet black or ash blonde) and has it cut in a short and deliberately tousled style. Both wear heavy black eye make-up and almost black lipstick.

Body The girl seated on the step wears very tight, short denim jeans with a bright yellow, leopard skin-printed top; her friend wears a tight black mini-skirt with sleeveless white top and scarlet fishnet tights. Although the clergyman appears to be conventionally dressed his dark, two-piece suit is rather disconcertingly very smartly cut, with the trousers fitting tightly over the hips and flaring a little towards the hem.

Accessories The girl on the right wears a choker, belt and wristband of studded leather and black, high-heeled ankle boots; the other has on low-heeled, white court shoes.

139 Midi-skirt, New York, 1970
The Sunday Times

Note A woman in a midi-length skirt stares at a placard in a shop window denouncing the fashion as 'Ugly. We won't Sell These'. Devotees of the mini-skirt were fighting a losing battle for its preservation in the early 1970s.

Head Her hair is worn long and loose but curls are now acceptable.

Body She wears a short, battledress-style jacket in leather (or imitation leather) and a mid-calf-length, gored skirt of checked cloth.

Accessories Her leather shoulder bag is decorated with applied star motifs and long, fringed stripes inspired by the U.S. national flag (an American version of the 1960s British fashion for using the Union flag as a decorative motif). She wears bar shoes with wedge heels.

137 Young Man, 1969–71
J. Davies

Head The figure has straight hair in a ragged-looking 'pudding basin' cut which covers the ears and back of the neck.

Body He is dressed in a checked tweed sports jacket, dark tapered trousers, white shirt and tie – the conventional, semi-formal day wear for men at this date.

138 Mr and Mrs Clark and Percy, 1970–1
D. Hockney

See colour plate, between pp. 120 and 121.

140 Tony Blackburn, 1971 BBC

Note A BBC publicity photograph of the Radio 1 Disc Jockey who introduced his own early morning programme from Monday to Friday.

Head His hair is worn in a long fringe (a style popularized by the Beatles some eight years earlier) and covers his ears. He also wears long side burns.

Body His patterned shirt, with tie to match, has long rounded collar points; his trousers are tailored in striped cloth and are tight-fitting.

Accessories He wears a large ring on the little finger of his left hand.

141 Dress by Bill Gibb, modelled by Twiggy, 1971
The Sunday Times

Note The British designer Bill Gibb (born 1943) responded to the new taste for romantic and ethnic clothes in the early 1970s. In this example he was clearly inspired by the folk costume of some European or Near Eastern country but there is also a feeling of nostalgia for the dress of an earlier historical period with the full-length skirt and slashed sleeves. Gibb pioneered the use of several different patterned fabrics in one costume – often putting a geometrical with a floral design – an idea which became very popular during the decade.

Head She wears a close-fitting, crocheted wool cap with multiple, uncut strings.

Body Her dress is in several parts: a voluminous, long-sleeved blouse gathered up and billowing out beneath a very short-waisted and tight-fitting jacket with long, split sleeves fastening with long ribbon ties; the ankle-length skirt is accordion-pleated.

Accessories She has horizontally striped stockings and sandals with high, wedge heels and thick, platform soles (which came into general fashion in 1970–71).

142 Zandra Rhodes, 1971
The Sunday Times

Note Zandra Rhodes (born 1940) was one of Britain's most original dress designers in the 1970s evolving a distinctive style of her own and exploring new ideas and directions. She was the first designer to absorb elements of the 'Punk' style into high fashion later in the decade.

Head Her collar-length, straight hair is razor cut and lifted at the crown to give a spiky effect (uncannily echoed by the plant behind her).

Body She wears loose-fitting denim dungarees with the hems rolled up above the ankle and a cotton blouse with full, bishop sleeves.

Accessories She has a large necklace like a garland round her neck and a number of fancy brooches attached to the bib front of her dungarees. Her ankle-strap sandals have high heels and ridged platform soles applied with glitter.

143 The Doobie Brothers, 1972
Warner/Reprise publicity photograph

Note The seven men in this American pop group
reflect the influence of the Hippy movement on
fashion of the late 1960s and early 1970s although
most of them wear the recognized uniform of the
young: blue denim jeans and casual shirts. Long
hair with a centre parting, beards and moustaches,
metal-rimmed spectacles, flower-patterned
garments and ethnic clothes were all associated
with the Hippies or Flower Children who were
'dropping out' of society at this period. Other
elements of fashionable dress can also be found
here: long, flared trousers, romantic dress (in the
form of historic revivals, for example the frilled
jabot and wrist ruffles, second from the left) and
the beret (third right) popularly connected with
Che Guevara, the South American guerrilla leader
and cult figure.

Head There is a wide variety of hair lengths in
this picture, ranging from the relatively short to
the extremely long (reflecting perhaps a general
uncertainty and policy of 'anything goes' in the
first years of the decade). But whatever its length
and style the hair is evidently well cared-for. Every
one of the figures wears a moustache or beard – the
moustaches mostly long and drooping in the
fashionable 'Mexican' style.

Body The men are all dressed casually in open-
necked shirts (having firmly rejected the tie, seen
as one of the badges of convention), waistcoats or
informal jackets, 'hipster' jeans or trousers and
either cowboy boots or training shoes. The
trousers on the left illustrate the extreme form of
the fashion for a very tight cut over the hips and
thighs, flaring widely from the knees to hems
which almost sweep the ground. The sharp centre
crease of conventional trousers has been
abandoned and the hip-level waistband with a
deep, buckled belt are usual. The vertical,
'handwarmer' pockets of the jacket on the far right
are a new alternative to pockets made useless by
the tight fit of the jeans.

Accessories For the same reason, keys are often
worn outside the pockets and can be attached by a
clip to the belt (second left).

**144 Baron Redcliffe-
Maud, 1972–3**
R. Spear

Note A portrait of the
distinguished diplomat
and academic Baron
Redcliffe-Maud (born
1906) in the correct but
now somewhat old-
fashioned formal day
dress for professional
men in town.

Head He wears a soft
felt trilby hat.

Body His black jacket
is in the lounge style
and is worn with a
double-breasted,
shawl-collared
waistcoat and grey
striped trousers. His
shirt has a low, narrow
collar, the points set at
an oblique angle.

Accessories His
pocket watch chain is
visible across his
waistcoat and he wears
a white handkerchief in
his breast pocket. He
carries two of the
professional man's
most familiar
accessories: a tightly-
furled umbrella and a
brief case.

125

145 Georgia, 1973
E. Uglow

Head The sitter's straight, dark hair hangs to her shoulders from a centre parting.

Body She wears a long, thigh-length tunic with high round neck and long sleeves, over trousers. These tunics, which were fashionable with trousers in the early 1970s, looked very similar to the mini-dresses of the late 1960s – indeed some actually were dresses and were worn either on their own or with trousers during this period of uncertainty about the exact level of the hemline.

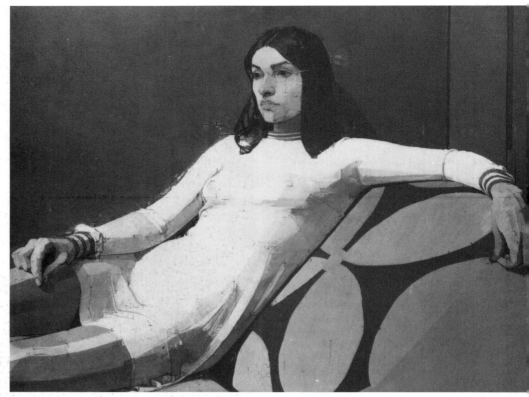

146 Mad Don of the Hollyhocks verging on the Rocks, 1974
T. Wright

Head The sitter's hair is cut in a long, graduated style covering the ears and reaching the shoulders at the back. He wears a wide-brimmed light straw trilby slouched over the eyes. American 'gangster' style hats of the 1930s were a fashionable revival at this date (see for example no. 69).

Body He is dressed in a plain, white, short-sleeved T-shirt and tailored cloth trousers with turned-up hems. The cut of the trouser legs is evidently long and flared, the outline of his long boots can be seen beneath.

Accessories He wears long, leather cowboy boots with high heels and platform soles. He has a wide tooled leather wrist band on one arm and wears a wedding ring.

147 Skinheads, *c.* **1975**
D. W. Ridgers

Note The Skinheads emerged as a young, mainly
working-class movement with a distinct new
image at the very end of the 1960s. Like the Mods
and Rockers of the earlier 1960s the Skinheads
were involved in violence and gang warfare but
this younger generation evolved a philosophy and
uniform of its own which made it immediately
recognizable.

Head The boys all have very short crewcuts.
Sometimes the hair was completely shaved, giving
rise to the name Skinhead (around 1969). The
haircut and facial expression were important
elements in the Skinhead image of aggression.

Body The Skinhead uniform consisted of an
open-necked shirt, braces and shortened trousers
or jeans with straight-fitting legs and turn-ups well
above the ankle. These were combined with heavy,
laced, army-issue type boots usually known as
'bovver' boots or 'Doc Martens'. Like the
crewcuts, this solid footwear gave a quasi-military
impression and was in fact used as a weapon to
kick both people and objects during violent
confrontations. Each boy has a dark jacket which
has been tied round the waist by its arms.

Accessories The boys are wearing badges
proclaiming their allegiance to some minority cult.
Many Skinheads became associated with the
National Front, a political organisation with
extreme reactionary views, and the black arm
bands with Union flag badges also worn by the
boys suggest this.

148 Boy's clothes by Viyella, 1976
William Hollins & Co. Ltd

Note Children's clothes still reflect adult fashions although brighter colours and bolder patterns are considered possible for the young. Boys are now wearing long trousers rather than shorts from an early age.

Head The boy's hair is cut with a long fringe and is shaped over the ears into the nape of the neck.

Body He wears a multicolour checked shirt in a polyester and cotton mixture. The long, flared trousers are of cotton printed in an imitation of patchwork. There was a great revival of interest in the traditional craft of patchwork in the early 1970s which led to the production of patchwork-printed textiles; denim jeans could also have applied patches (more often decorative than real).

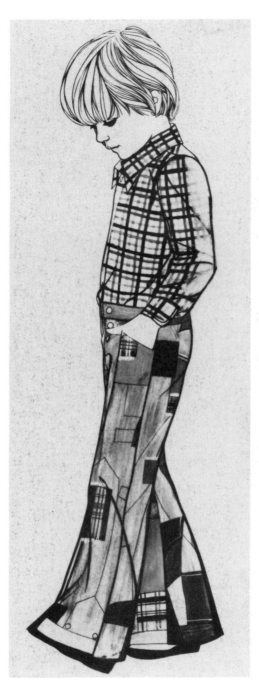

149 Young Worker, 1976
D. Hanson

Note Duane Hanson's realistic sculpture portrays a young American workman, but his appearance could equally well be that of any young workman in the Western hemisphere at this time. It was a look that had become a virtual uniform for young people and most students.

Head His untidy, collar-length hair covers the ears.

Body He wears a short-sleeved, round-necked T-shirt over well-worn, faded, blue denim jeans cut with a slight flare at the hem. Flared trousers were now reaching the end of their life and after 1976 there was a return to the straight-legged shape.

Accessories His heavy shoes are strapped over the instep. His wrist watch has a wide leather strap.

150 Shirt dress by Kenzo Takada of 'Jap', 1977

Note The Dress of the Year 1977 at the Museum of Costume in Bath was a shirt dress by Kenzo Takada (born 1940), one of the most influential young designers working in Paris in the 1970s. Kenzo was one of several Japanese designers to challenge the established cut and shape of clothes and to introduce ideas based on the traditional clothing of the Near and Far East. In 1977 he showed his new 'sack' which revived the 1960s mini-skirt, but in a new form.

Head The display mannequin by Adel Rootstein is modelled with oriental features, a type of beauty which was now becoming admired, and the hair is long and straight.

Body The dress is short and full, cut like a man's tunic-style shirt with turn-down collar and dolman sleeves, in khaki cotton poplin. It is bloused over a narrow, plaited leather belt round the hips.

Accessories She wears a plaited straw trilby hat, fawn knitted cotton ankle socks and canvas laced shoes. (The floral garland round her neck was a display accessory.)

129

151 My Parents, 1977
D. Hockney

Note Hockney's double portrait illustrates the conservative style of dress worn by an elderly couple.

Head Mrs Hockney's white hair is loosely waved and brushed back from her face. Her husband's hair is short at the back and sides.

Body She wears a plain, high-necked and long-sleeved dress just reaching the knee. He is in a dark, three-piece lounge suit.

Accessories Hockney's mother wears low-heeled shoes with broad, rounded toes; his father wears elastic-sided boots which had become fashionable for young men in the 1960s.

**152 Clothes by Simpson (Piccadilly) Ltd,
Autumn 1978**
E. Stemp

Note In the later 1970s a longer, looser cut
became fashionable for women, with an emphasis
on separates and layers of garments.

Head The women's hair is arranged in rather
shorter, neater styles than earlier in the decade.

Body The man is dressed in a brown polo-necked
sweater, cavalry twill trousers and oatmeal tweed
safari jacket by Daks. The women wear calf-
length, circular cut tweed skirts – on the left
teamed with a checked shirt, knitted waistcoat and
cardigan, on the right with a polo-necked sweater
and blouson jacket.

Accessories High-heeled knee boots are
fashionable wear at this date with both skirts and
dresses.

153 Dress by Calvin Klein, 1980

Note A dress by the American designer Calvin Klein (born 1942) was chosen as the Dress of the Year 1980 for the Museum of Costume in Bath. American designers were beginning to make an impact on European high fashion with their talent for easy, understated elegance.

Head The model's hair is cut in a short, sporty style that looks both natural and sleek.

Body She wears a sleeveless, wrap-over dress of dark red and brown striped silk crêpe de chine with a broad tie belt of burgundy and bronze leather. The dress is intended to be suitable for a number of different social occasions and for women of different ages. The designer sees the wearer herself moulding the dress to her own requirements rather than the dress imposing the shape of fashion on her.

Accessories Her earrings, necklace and bracelets are of natural wood. She wears narrow-strapped, high-heeled sandals of burgundy leather.

154 Alec Douglas-Home, 1980
S. Malin

Note A relaxed portrait of the Conservative politician and former Prime Minister, Alec Douglas–Home (born 1903). Although he is clearly dressed for fishing in this picture, Lord Home's clothes would hardly look out of place for informal daytime wear in London and are almost dateless, representing a classic style of dress for men which has come to be regarded as particularly English.

Body He wears a checked tweed sports jacket and cloth trousers with a checked shirt and paisley-patterned tie – a form of dress usual for country pursuits.

133

134

155 Diana, Princess of Wales, 1981
B. Organ

Note Following her marriage to Prince Charles in 1981, at the age of 20, the Princess of Wales became greatly admired throughout the world for her natural good looks and youthful, stylish taste in clothes. In this deliberately informal portrait she not only wears trousers but sits with her legs crossed and gazes out at the spectator with poise, breaking with the usual traditions of royal portraiture.

Head Her blonde hair is cut short but is worn in a long fringe swept across her forehead and over her ears. This hairstyle was not originated by the Princess but became as completely associated with her as the fringe worn by her predecessor, Princess Alexandra, 100 years earlier.

Body She wears a high-necked, frilled blouse worn open at the neck, with a black waistcoat trimmed with gold braid, and matching trousers, tapered and turned up at the ankle.

Accessories She has on several pieces of gold jewellery: hoop earrings, bracelet and rings. Her shoes are plain, black, low-heeled pumps.

156 Lord Volvo and his Estate, 1982
H. Ocean

Note A group of young men in casual dress. These clothes reflect not only the influence of recent teenage cults such as the Punks and the earlier Skinheads, but also a revival, in the early 1980s, of working-class teenage styles of the 1950s and 1960s.

Head Most of the men have short hair. The man by the car on the left has the long quiff and side burns reminiscent of the Teddy Boy style of the 1950s; Lord Volvo's hair is shaved short with the suggestion of a 'Mohican' plume, a reminder of both Punk and Skinhead haircuts.

Body Almost all the men wear denim jeans (which have now been popular with young people for over 20 years) and these are close-fitting and straight-legged. They are worn with T-shirts, shirts, sweaters and casual jackets. Lord Volvo however has on a checked, two-piece lounge suit, but its superficially conventional appearance is belied by the short trouser legs with turn-ups (favoured by the Skinheads a decade earlier) and the tartan scarf tucked into the jacket – an echo of the traditional working-man's muffler (see for example no. 51). The reclining man to his left wears a red and yellow 'psychedelic' patterned shirt in the style of the later 1960s.

Accessories The man on the far left sports a number of badges on his waistcoat; his neighbour wears a pull-on knitted hat. Lord Volvo's heavy, laced shoes are very similar to the Skinhead 'bovver' boots (see also no. 147). Behind him one young man wears side-laced shoes with very pointed toes, again a revival of the 1950s and the 'winklepicker' style.

157 Match of the Day, 1982
S. Rossberg

See colour plate, between pp. 120 and 121.

158 Boys in 'Boy', 1983
S. Rossberg

Note The avant-garde clothes shop 'Boy' appeared in the King's Road, London in the later 1970s.

Head Three very different styles of hair are illustrated here. The boy in the foreground owes something to the Punk image with the head shaved at the sides to leave a shock of spiky hair on the crown; behind him on the left the man has longer hair, deliberately untidy but with feminine undertones which contrast provocatively with his muscular build. The man on the right has an aggressively masculine, quasi-military short cut. The figure on the far left, in a beret, is neither recognizably male or female.

Body The figure in the foreground wears denim jeans and jacket intentionally crumpled and worn, but both his T-shirt and those of his companions have obviously been designed with care. The shelves behind are piled with patterned T-shirts.

Accessories Studded leather wristbands are on the counter for sale. The man on the far right wears a digital watch with metal strap.

159 Jogging suits, 1983
Men's Wear magazine

Note An interest in physical fitness encouraged
many people to take up jogging and manufacturers
began producing a whole new range of sportswear
to meet this enthusiasm.

Head The man's hair is short; the woman's is
shoulder-length and left loose, emphasizing the
attraction of clean, healthy and natural looking
hair.

Body Both wear smart jogging suits in white with
contrasting cuffs and waistbands. Based on the
traditional tracksuit for athletics, the jogging suit
of knitted cotton with fleecy lining provides
warmth and cover while allowing complete
freedom of movement. However, the original
shapelessness of the trousers has been altered here
to create a more flattering fit over the hips and
thighs.

Accessories They wear light running shoes to
match.

160 Casual clothes by Lee Cooper Italia, 1983
G. Villa

Note Although denim jeans continued to be popular with both men and women in the early 1980s they were less universally worn than in the 1970s. The shape changed and a straight, very narrow fit was fashionable. A similarity between male and female dress is noticeable with the garments appearing virtually interchangeable.

Head Hair is fairly short and left to look as natural and as casual as possible.

Body Both figures wear loose-fitting, chunky sweaters over slim-fitting jeans. The wide-shouldered waistcoat worn by the young man would be equally appropriate wear for the girl.

Accessories Both wear long scarves either left hanging loose or negligently knotted round the neck; both have on wedge-soled, laced sports shoes.

161 Smoking – study in Greys, 1984
P. Barton

Note Although the Punk style had made its point
and ceased to shock by the early 1980s it was kept
alive by small groups of young people in most
provincial British towns.

Head The young men here wear two of the most
familiar Punk hair styles – either a halo of stiffened
spikes or a 'Mohican' plume (with the sides of the
head shaved bare).

Body Their clothes are a modified version of
Punk garments: they wear black leather jackets
with metal studs on the collar, shoulders and
sleeves, with tight, patched and torn jeans.

Accessories Two of the youths have badges
pinned to their jackets (almost certainly one of the
badges is for the Campaign for Nuclear
Disarmament). A third wears fingerless mittens.

**162 Clothes by Katharine Hamnett, Betty Jackson and Body Map,
1984**
Wessex Newspapers

Note The clothes were chosen for the Museum of Costume's Dress of the
Year collection in 1984 and reflect the influence of 'street fashion' on
contemporary dress design.

Head The man's hair is short at the sides but swept back over the crown
rather in the manner of the American college boy of the 1950s. Both the girls
wear hats. The model on the right has eyebrows and lips painted white.

Body The man models Katharine Hamnett's comfortable clothes for men:
thin silk, loose-fitting jacket and trousers with a large cotton T-shirt (printed
with a political slogan) and a cotton shirt knotted round the waist. In the
centre is Betty Jackson's long, tube-like dress and jacket of striped, knitted
wool with a printed wool scarf. On the right the model wears Body Map's
long top and fluted skirt patterned to match the hat.

Accessories All three wear flat, comfortable shoes – the women's appearing
to have taken over men's styles (worn with ankle socks or striped stockings).

163 Skiwear by Head, 1985

Note The second half of the 1980s was to see a new image for men: more health conscious, sensitive and caring. Although success at work was still recognised as important by many, time spent with the family and in enjoyment of children was often emphasised. Sports clothes were still an important element of fashion and gave an interchangeable nature to both adults' and children's clothes.

Head The man's hair is short and well-groomed, giving an appearance of cleanliness and good health. The pull-on knitted caps are practical accessories for skiing but are also worn by children with ordinary outdoor wear.

Body The padded anorak jackets, trousers and ski suit reflect the shape of current fashion with their easy cut and straight, slim legs. Ski clothes, like other sportswear, were carefully designed to be both functional and stylish. The smart appearance of many jackets led to their adoption for other sporting or casual wear.

164 Woman's and Man's clothes by Giorgio Armani, 1986

Note Giorgio Armani (born 1935) is an Italian designer with an international reputation for well cut and tailored clothes in the classical tradition but adapted to the needs of modern social and business life. In the design-conscious decade of the 1980s his suits became a status symbol for affluent young working men and women – what came to be known as *power dressing*.

Head The woman's hair is sleekly drawn back to complement the streamlined appearance of her clothes. The man's hair is short at the back but worn long over the crown, greased and combed straight back.

Body The collarless tweed jacket on the left, checked in black, white and grey, has extremely wide, padded shoulders. It is worn over a plain grey silk blouse and a grey herringbone weave wool skirt with a gathered waist and long hemline reaching well below the knee. The man is more casually dressed in a knitted silk shirt and wool tie, blue tweed jacket and black corduroy trousers.

Accessories The woman's shoes are low-heeled court shoes in black suede; the man's are dark brown polished leather with crepe rubber soles.

**165 Coat and skirt by John Galliano, 1987
Drawing by C. Smalley**

Note John Galliano (born 1960), a British fashion
designer, was inspired by the layered and draped
effects of later eighteenth century dress in his 1987
collections. His work was hailed for its unorthodox
cut and treatment of different garments. The soft,
fanciful line and elongated shaping of this dress
contrasts with the more structured and sharply
styled clothes favoured by mainstream fashion in
the mid 1980s. It represents an alternative manner
of dressing favoured by younger and less
conventional women.

Head Firmly controlled hair in a neat coil and a
spiky hat are unexpectedly combined with the
billowing shapes of the coat and skirt.

Body A very high-waisted skirt, slightly bunched
over the hips to break the flow towards the hem, is
worn under a jacket or open-front overdress
draped in the manner of an eighteenth-century
polonaise skirt.

Accessories Beneath the long skirt, thick ribbed
woollen stockings or tights are worn with flat-
heeled, lace-up shoes.

Modesty Blaze

166 Suit by Lolita Lempicka, 1987

Note The tailored suit became very fashionable for women during the later 1980s both for professional and social occasions. This seemed to meet a need, particularly on the part of the growing number of working women, to project a competent yet feminine image (exemplified perhaps by the then Prime Minister, Margaret Thatcher).

By 1987 short skirts had returned to fashion but the new length differed from the 1960s mini-skirt in being cut very straight and tight. Their effect depended on the possession of long legs and slender thighs – a continuation of the decade's emphasis on a slim, fit body.

Head The woman's hair, cut in a short straight bob with a fringe, complements the line of the suit and helps to create a sleek and glossy appearance.

Body The potentially masculine features of the scarlet cloth jacket – wide lapels, square shoulders and double-breasted fastening – have been modified by a shaped waistline and a fluted peplum over the hips. The straight skirt is worn several inches above the knee and it was now usual to emphasise the legs with dark sheer or opaque tights.

Accessories The new short skirt is worn here with high heeled and pointed court shoes. The model wears leather gloves although these were not regarded as an essential accessory. However, flamboyant costume jewellery was an element of this look and in this example consists of large pearl and gold clip earrings and a diamond-studded gold bracelet.

167 Man's suit by Next, 1988

Note The Next chain of clothes shops for men and women were a phenomenal success of the 1980s. Under the direction of George Davies they provided fashionable, well made but reasonably priced clothes which were sold in smartly designed shops. In 1988 the mail order catalogue Next Directory was launched, extending the range of goods still further. Amongst other items, Next offered a relatively inexpensive version of the classic bespoke suit which was fashionable once again for business wear. In this illustration the Next catalogue appeals to a younger generation of men but reflects a fashionably nostalgic view of traditional British tailoring in an old world country house setting.

Head Longer hair, greased and combed straight back (as in 164) is still fashionable.

Body The model wears a two-piece business suit tailored in a navy wool and polyester mix flannel. It has a double-breasted jacket and easy fitting trousers with turn-ups. The plain cream shirt and blue/grey striped tie underline the traditional appearance of the suit but with the intention of creating an effect which is young and smart rather than dull and conventional.

Accessories Other classic accessories include dark ribbed socks, black brogued Oxford shoes and a wrist watch with a leather strap.

168 Woman's clothes by Next, 1988

Note This Next Directory illustration reflects the continuing popularity of separates (garments such as a blazer-style jacket, blouse and patterned skirt). The idea of mixing and matching items to create an outfit had become widespread some ten years earlier. Like 167 the photographer has created a nostalgic image of an earlier period: in this case the 1950s, with the model's stylized pose, dark glasses and vanity case.

Head The hair is cut short and carefully shaped to sweep back off the face in a naturally windswept manner.

Body Although the jacket, pleated skirt and white blouse are 'classic' pieces designed to look like natural fibres they include a large percentage of man-made material (which obviously made them moderately priced and easier to care for). The navy double-breasted blazer is tailored in a wool and polyester mix garbardine, the navy and cream plaid skirt is a polyester 'crepe de Chine' and the linen look blouse is a ramie and polyester mix.

Accessories The black sunglasses, broad belt and flat heeled loafer shoes were also available by mail order.

169 Suit by Romeo Gigli, 1990

Note   This velvet trouser suit and silk organza
blouse by the Italian designer Romeo Gigli was
chosen as the Dress of the Year for the Museum of
Costume in Bath. It shows a move away from the
hard-edged shapes and executive-style suits of the
1980s towards a softer, more traditionally feminine
line: more natural shoulders, fluid fabrics and
subtle colours. This was perceived as a less
aggressive image for women as the decade opened.

Head   The model's long, straight hair is parted
and drawn back smoothly into a coil at the nape of
the neck.

Body   The suit of two-tone midnight blue and
black silk velvet has a four-button cutaway jacket
cut like a man's morning coat. The trousers are
high waisted, slim and tapered. These are worn
with a scarf-necked blouse in shaded silk organza
and a deep cummerbund of dark green wool
embroidered in coloured silks and gold thread.

Accessories   The model wears front lacing ankle
boots of black leather.

170 'Going Green', autumn/winter 1990–91

Note Although this feature was published in the trade journal *Fashion Weekly* in July 1989 it forecasts commercial trends for the following winter 1990–91. It is a review of 'Expofil', the French Yarn Show which brings together designers, weavers, knitters, manufacturers and retailers and attracts visitors on an international scale. 'Ecology and all things natural was the overall feeling at the fair' it says and this reflects the growing concern in the early 1990s with 'green' issues of conservation and a respect for the environment.

Head The women's hairstyles illustrated here are mostly long but smoothed back off the face and knotted at the back of the head.

Body The sketches of style predictions show for men a continuation of the shape fashionable in the late 1980s – roomy coats and jackets, easy fitting trousers and sporting garments adapted for leisure wear. For women, shorts and dark tights or narrow trousers worn with short A-line jackets are featured together with the alternative long skirt and soft, layered look. All these garments, they suggest, are made from natural fibres or fabrics which look natural in earthy browns, and greens and 'autumnal' colours and with textured surfaces like tweeds and ribbed or herringbone weaves.

Accessories The women's shoes are generally flat or low-heeled.

Select Bibliography

The following publications deal with fashionable dress and accessories. Articles on specific aspects of twentieth-century dress and reviews of new publications and exhibitions can be found in *Costume*, the annual journal of the Costume Society; *Textile History*, a bi-annual journal published by the Pasold Research Fund; and *Dress*, the annual journal of the Costume Society of America.

Alexander, H., *Fans*. The Costume Accessories Series, Batsford, 1984

Arnold, J., *Patterns of Fashion*, vol. II (*c*. 1860—1940), Macmillan, 1972

Baines, B., *Fashion Revivals from the Elizabethan Age to the Present Day*, Batsford, 1981

Battersby, M., *The Decorative Twenties*, Studio Vista, 1969
The Decorative Thirties, Studio Vista, 1971

Beaton, C., *The Glass of Fashion*, Weidenfeld & Nicolson, 1954

Bernard, B., *Fashion in the Sixties*, Academy Editions, 1978

Bowman, S., *A Fashion for Extravagance: Art Déco Fabrics and Fashions*, Bell & Hyman, 1985

Byrde, P., *The Male Image: Men's Fashions in Britain 1300–1970*, Batsford, 1979

Carnegy, V., *Fashions of a Decade: The 1980s*, Batsford, 1990

Carter, E., *The Changing World of Fashion*, Weidenfeld & Nicolson, 1977
Magic Names of Fashion, Weidenfeld & Nicolson, 1980

Charles-Roux, E., *Chanel and Her World*, Weidenfeld & Nicolson, 1981

Clark, F., *Hats*. The Costume Accessories Series, Batsford, 1982

Cohn, N., *Today There Are No Gentlemen*, Weidenfeld & Nicolson, 1971

Coleridge, N., *The Fashion Conspiracy: from sweatshop to couture – a journey into the interior*, Heinemann, 1988

Connikie, Y., *Fashions of a Decade: The 1960s*, Batsford, 1990

Cumming, V., *Gloves*. The Costume Accessories Series, Batsford, 1982
The Royal Image: royalty and its clothing 1580 to the present day, Batsford, 1989

De La Haye, A., *Fashion Source Book: a visual reference to twentieth century fashion design*, Macdonald Orbis, 1988

De Marly, D., *The History of Haute Couture 1850–1950*, Batsford, 1980
Fashion for Men. An Illustrated History, Batsford, 1985
Christian Dior, Batsford, 1989

Demornex, J., *Balenciaga*, Thames & Hudson, 1989

Deslandres, Y., *Paul Poiret*, Thames & Hudson, 1987

Dorner, J., *Fashion in the Twenties and Thirties*, Ian Allan, 1973
Fashion in the Forties and Fifties, Ian Allan, 1975

Ewing, E., *History of Twentieth Century Fashion*, Batsford, rev. ed., 1992
Dress and Undress. A History of Women's Underwear, Batsford, 1978

Foster, V., *Bags and Purses*. The Costume Accessories Series, Batsford, 1982

Giroud, F., *Dior*, Thames & Hudson, 1987

Glynn, P., and Ginsburg, M., *In Fashion; Dress in the Twentieth Century*, Allen & Unwin, 1978

Howell, G., *In Vogue. Six Decades of Fashion*, Allen Lane, 1975, new ed. Century and Condé Nast, 1991

Keenan, B., *Dior in Vogue*, Octopus Books, 1981

Langbridge, R. H., (Ed.), *Edwardian Shopping. A Selection from the Army and Navy Stores catalogues 1893–1913*, David & Charles, 1975

Laver, J., *Women's Dress in the Jazz Age*, Hamish Hamilton, 1964

Lee-Potter, C., *Sportswear in Vogue since 1910*, Thames & Hudson, 1984

Lurie, A., *The Language of Clothes*, Heinemann, 1981

McDowell, C., *McDowell's Directory of Twentieth Century Fashion*, Frederick Muller, 1984.
Shoes: fashion and fantasy, Thames & Hudson, 1989

Mackrell, A., *Poiret*, Batsford, 1989

Mansfield, A., and Cunnington, P., *Handbook of English Costume in the Twentieth Century 1900–1950*, Faber, 1973

Martin, R., *Fashion and Surrealism*, Thames & Hudson, 1988

Milbank, C. R., *Couture: the great fashion designers*, Thames & Hudson, 1985

Moore, D. L., *Fashion Through Fashion Plates 1771–1970*, Ward, Lock, 1971

Mulvagh, J., *The Vogue History of Twentieth Century Fashion*, Viking, 1988

O'Hara, G., *The Encyclopaedia of Fashion*, Thames & Hudson, 1986

Probert, C., *Shoes in Vogue since 1910*, Thames & Hudson, 1981
Hats in Vogue since 1910, Thames & Hudson, 1981
Lingerie in Vogue since 1910, Thames & Hudson, 1981
Swimwear in Vogue since 1910, Thames & Hudson, 1981
Brides in Vogue since 1910, Thames & Hudson, 1984

Quant, M., *Quant by Quant*, Cassell, 1966

Ribeiro, A., *Dress and Morality*, Batsford, 1986, 1990

Robinson, J., *The Golden Age of Style*, Orbis Books, 1976
Fashion in the Thirties, Oresko Books, 1978
Fashion in the Forties, Academy Editions, 1976

Ross, J., *Royalty in Vogue, 1909–1989*, Chatto, 1989

Scarisbrick, D., *Jewellery*. The Costume Accessories Series, Batsford, 1984

Steele, V., *Paris Fashion: mode and meaning in the capital of style*, Oxford University Press, 1988

Stevenson, P., *Edwardian Fashion*, Ian Allan, 1980

Swann, J., *Shoes*. The Costume Accessories Series, Batsford, 1982

Vreeland, D., *Inventive Paris Clothes 1909–1939*, Thames & Hudson, 1978

Walkley, C., *The Way to Wear 'em: 150 Years of PUNCH on Fashion*, Peter Owen, 1985

Waugh, N., *The Cut of Women's Clothes 1600–1930*, Faber, 1968

White, P., *Poiret*, Studio Vista, 1973
Elsa Schiaparelli, Aurum Press, 1986

Wilson, W., and Taylor, L., *Through the Looking Glass: a history of dress from 1860 to the present day*, BBC Publications, 1989

York, P., *Style Wars*, Sidgwick & Jackson, 1980

Exhibition catalogues and museum publications:

Brighton Museum
Mariano Fortuny 1871–1949, exhibition catalogue, 1980

Brighton Museum and Bath Museum of Costume
Norman Hartnell, 1985

Leeds Art Galleries
Jean Muir, 1980

Museum of London
Mary Quant's London, exhibition catalogue, 1973

Manchester City Art Galleries
Women's Costume 1900–1930, 1956
20th century Fashion, 1979

Manchester Whitworth Art Gallery (with Trefoil Books, 1986)
1966 and All That. Design and the Consumer in Britain 1960–1969

Scottish Arts Council
Fashion 1900–1939, exhibition catalogue, 1975

Victoria and Albert Museum, London
Fashion: an anthology by Cecil Beaton, exhibition catalogue, 1971
Liberty's 1875–1975, exhibition catalogue, 1975
Four Hundred Years of Fashion (published by Collins), 1983
Twentieth Century: an introduction to women's fashionable dress 1900–1980, 1983

Glossary and Select Index

Note   This list is designed to serve as both a Glossary and an Index. Some entries include definitions of costume and textile terms which are not fully explained in either the text or captions; those which have been explained already are merely indexed. The numbers in brackets refer to the plates where selected examples of the items listed can be studied. (Certain items, such as women's suits, men's lounge suits, knitwear, and handbags appear too frequently to be included in this system). The names of dress designers whose work is illustrated in the plates have also been mentioned.

Armani, Giorgio (164)

Artistic dress (28) (40) (119)

Backcombing A technique to give the hair fullness and height by combing a lock at a time in the reverse direction, towards the roots. (121) (122)

Bakst, Léon (30)

Bandeau A narrow band worn round the head, crossing the forehead just above the eyebrows. (39)

Bar shoe Fastening with one or more straps over the instep. (32) (56) (130) (139)

Bates, John (128) (131)

Bishop sleeve Full from the shoulder to the wrist where it is gathered into a close-fitting cuff. (142)

Boa A long, narrow stole or scarf, soft and round in shape, made of feathers or fur. It was worn throughout the nineteenth century but was especially fashionable in the 1890s. (93)

Boater Man's stiff straw hat with a flat, shallow crown and straight brim. (11)

Bolero jacket A short jacket, usually ending above the waist and worn open at the front. (13) (98)

Bonnet A small hat, usually with no brim at the back and tying under the chin with ribbon strings. (12) (17) (126)

Bowler hat Man's felt hat with a stiffened, domed crown and narrow, curled brim. (29) (49) (69) (96)

Box coat The term originally meant the heavy, caped overcoats worn by coachmen and travellers in the eighteenth and nineteenth century but when used in the 1930s and 1940s it refers to the fashionable boxy shape of women's coats with their padded, square shoulders and loose fit round the waist. (87)

Brilliantine A type of hair oil. (60)

Broderie anglaise Cutwork embroidery, usually in cotton; a pattern is made of small, round or oval holes which are cut and overcast, interspersed with motifs in satin stitch and stem stitch. (6) (27)

Brogued A form of decorating the shoe. The sections of the uppers have serrated edges, double-stitched seams and a pattern of small, punched holes. (103) (167)

Braid Flat, narrow strips of often coarsely woven fabric used for trimming. (11) (20)

Busk Long, flat, narrow piece of metal or whalebone inserted at the centre front of the corset to give it a rigid line.

Cap   A head-covering which is generally small, close-fitting and of soft material. A flat, tweed or cloth cap with stiffened visor appeared for sports wear in the late nineteenth century. Women's caps: (16) (17) (36) (41) (141). Men's caps: (17) (45) (51) (69)

Cardigan A jacket of knitted wool. (35) (53)

Chanel, Gabrielle (53)

Chemise A loose-fitting and unshaped undergarment of linen or cotton worn by all women until the end of the nineteenth century. In the twentieth century the term has been used as an adjective to describe dresses of a similar straight, loose cut. (44) (58)

Chesterfield A popular style of overcoat for men since the 1840s when it was named after the 6th Earl of Chesterfield, a fashionable figure in Society. The coat is fitted and slightly waisted, with the sleeves set in to a round armhole, and it usually has a velvet collar. (15) (49) (60)

Chignon An arrangement of hair at the back of the head. (4)

Chiffon A semi-transparent, light, thin silk. (7) (9) (66)

Choker necklace A close-fitting string of pearls, beads or stones worn round the base of the neck. (120 (93) (97) (106)

Cloche hat A bell-shaped hat with a deep crown and small brim, or no brim. (48) (53) (54) (55) (56)

Cloth Although the term is used for any woven fabric it normally refers to a closely-woven material of fine quality wool. (10) (12)

Corsage Originally meaning the upper part or bodice of a dress but used in the twentieth century to refer to a spray of real or artificial flowers worn on the bodice. (4)

Corset A tight-fitting, rigid undergarment moulding the figure and compressing the waist to the shape of fashion. (9) (31)

Courrèges, André (126)

150

Court dress A highly regulated, formal style of dress worn for Court functions and on presentation to the monarch. (14)

Court dressmaker A term used by leading dressmakers and fashion houses in the earlier twentieth century, implying that their clientèle came from the ranks of those who were presented at Court and that their standards of dressmaking were equal to the demands of such occasions; not that they supplied clothes to the Royal Family and immediate Court circle.

Court shoe A heeled shoe with plain, low-cut front. (24) (44) (80) (102) (164) (166)

Couture/Haute couture/couturier Couture: dressmaking (from the French for sewing). Haute couture: the design and making of fashionable clothes. Couturier/ière: dressmaker or dress designer.

Cravat Man's silk necktie folded or tied at the front. (33) (119)

Crêpe Usually a silk or woollen fabric with a crimped surface achieved by the use of a high-twist yarn. (59) (122)

Crêpe de Chine A fine, soft crêpe with a silk warp and weft. (39) (43) (153) (168)

Cuff-links A pair of discs, usually metal, joined by a link or short chain to fasten the split cuff or wristband of a man's shirt. Buttons or links have been in use since the late seventeenth century. (21) (127)

Cummerbund (127) (169)

Décolletage The low neckline of women's dress. (7)

Denim A twilled cotton fabric, used originally for working overalls but later universally adopted for men's, women's and children's jeans. (147) (149) (156) (157) (160) (161)

Dinner jacket/suit (60) (77) (96) (109) (127)

Directoire The period of government in France from 1795 to 1799. The term was used to describe the revival, in the first decade of the present century, of the style of dress of that era. See also *Empire line*. (22) (26) (30)

Dior, Christian (94) (108)

Doucet, Jacques (9)

Dress coat/suit (21) (60) (77)

Duffel/duffle coat A loose-fitting, hooded coat with double-breasted toggle fastenings, made of a thick woollen cloth with a nap. The cloth was originally produced in the Flemish town of Duffel. (119)

Dungarees Originally working men's overalls but taken up for fashionable women's wear in the 1970s in the form of loose-fitting jeans with a bib-fronted top. (142)

Empire line The distinctive style of dress associated with period of the French Empire under Napoleon I (1804–1814) when women's gowns had very short-waisted bodices and long, slim skirts. It is similar to the fashions of the French *Directoire* period which preceded the Empire and the English Regency period (1811–1820) by which names this line is also known. It has been fashionably revived several times during this century. (108) (130)

Eton suit Boy's suit with a short jacket, shirt with a wide, turned-over collar stiffly starched, waistcoat and long trousers. (24)

Fichu A light scarf or neckerchief worn round the neck and shoulders. (8) (70)

Flannel Woollen cloth in a plain or twill weave. (100) (167)

Fortuny, Mariano (40)

Fratini, Gina (134)

Frock coat (1) (10) (20)

Galliano, John (165)

Gauntlet gloves Gloves with deep cuffs covering the wrists. (16) (69) (78)

Georgette A thin silk fabric with a crêpe weave. (39)

Gibb, Bill (141)

Gigli, Romeo (169)

Hartnell, Norman (71)

Haute couture See *Couture*

Hobble skirt (26) (31) (32)

Homburg hat (1)

Incorporated Society of London Fashion Designers (88) (110)

Inverness A man's loose-fitting overcoat with a collar and shoulder cape. Particularly fashionable during the second half of the nineteenth century. (63)

Jabot A frill or ruffle, usually of lace, worn at the neck and decorating the front of the bodice. (26) (143)

Jeans (124) (138) (143). See also *Denim*.

Jumper suit (48) (53)

Kenzo Takada (150)

Klein, Calvin (153) (167)

Knickerbockers A form of men's breeches but cut several inches fuller and wider than ordinary knee breeches. They became popular for country and sporting wear in the later nineteenth century. An even looser, longer style (with the fullness overhanging the tops of the hose) which became fashionable in the 1920s were known as *plus fours* (q.v.). (45)

Louis heel High heel, waisted or curved inwards. (39) (43) (58)

Lucile (22)

Mannequin *1* A person (usually a woman) who displays clothes by wearing them. Generally known as a fashion model. (6) (95) (102) (122) (123) (129). *2* A lay figure or dummy used for the display of clothes in a shop or museum. (150) (153)

Marocain A silk or wool fabric with a crêpe weave. (48)

Moiré A water-marked effect, usually on silk, created by passing the fabric through engraved rollers. (129)

Molyneux, Edward (67)

Monocle Single eye-glass, usually suspended on a cord round the neck. (63)

Morning coat/suit (1) (20) (25) (31) (71) (169)

Motoring clothes (16)

Mourning (2)

Muir, Jean (135)

Muslin A general term for soft, light, openly-woven cotton fabrics. (8)

New Look (94) (95)

Norfolk suit A blouse-like jacket with cuffed sleeves, yoked and pleated at the front and back with a waist belt. Generally worn with knickerbockers (q.v.). (17)

Nylon The first synthetic fibre, discovered through research by the American chemical firm Du Pont. Commercial production in the USA began in 1939 and nylon stockings were available by 1940. It has been made in Britain since 1941 under the trade name Bri-nylon.

Oxford shoe Man's lace-up shoe. (103 167)

Panama hat Man's summer hat of fine, flexible straw, similar in shape to a trilby. (23)

Paquin, Madame (6) (30) (58)

Patou, Jean (59)

Picture hat A large, wide-brimmed woman's hat. (71) (102) (107)

Pinafore dress (123)

Platform shoe Shoes with an unusually deep sole and heel to correspond. These were fashionable during the 1940s and were then revived and taken to greater extremes in the early 1970s. (95) (102) (141) (142) (146)

Plus fours A style of knickerbockers (q.v.) popular for golfing wear in the 1920s and 1930s. The term may derive from the extra four inches in length which gave the breeches the requisite fullness over the knees but it is also said to come from a golfing expression. (45)

Pochoir From the French term for stencil, a process by which a monochrome print is coloured by hand using a series of stencils. (30) (44)

Poiret, Paul (19)

Poplin A strong, smooth fabric, originally with a silk warp and worsted weft but later also made of cotton. (150)

Pumps Flat or low-heeled shoes with soft, low-cut uppers. (27) (112) (132) (155)

Punk (156) (157) (161)

Quant, Mary (123) (129)

Quiff A lock of hair either pressed down over the forehead or brushed up from the brow. (114) (156)

Raglan sleeve A wide sleeve, not set into a round armhole but tapering to a point at the neckband. (49) (69)

Rhodes, Zandra (142)

Roll collar A curved, turned-back collar cut in one with the lapels (i.e. with no notch). (75) (127)

Sailor suit A popular form of dress for children consisting of a sailor's blouse with a wide, turned-back collar and long trousers (or pleated skirt for girls). (17) (24)

Satin A silk fabric with a smooth, glossy face. (59) (98)

Schiaparelli, Elsa (78)

Shantung silk A plain weave cloth of wild or slubbed silk (i.e. with surface irregularities). (108)

Shawl collar Similar to a roll collar (q.v.) but usually deeper. (1) (59)

Shelter/siren suit (84)

Shorts (women's) (129) (170)

Side-burns Men's short side whiskers. Named after the American General Burnside *c.* 1875. Known as 'burnsides' in the USA and also called 'sideboards' in the UK. (140) (156)

Sling-back shoe An open-heeled shoe. (103)

Slip *1* A man's white under-waistcoat, the top edge of which showed above the waistcoat. (10). *2* Twentieth-century term for a woman's petticoat or undergarment worn with an unlined dress or skirt. (57)

Slipper An indoor shoe, flat, low-cut and easy-fitting. (85) (117)

Spats A short gaiter or covering for the ankle made of white or light-coloured canvas, buttoning on the outer side and with a strap passing under the foot. (33) (49)

Sports dress (8) (17) (45) (74) (98) (154) (159) (163) (170)

Sports jacket (44) (100) (113) (137) (154)

Stiebel, Victor (122)

Stiletto shoe A shoe with a very narrow heel like a metal spike or stiletto. (115) (118) (121)

Stole A long scarf or shawl worn over the shoulders. (50)

T-shirt An informal shirt or top with a round neck and short sleeves, made of jersey-knit cotton. (146) (149) (156) (158) (162)

Tea gown (9)

Terylene Trade name for the polyester fibre first discovered in 1941 and produced in the UK by I.C.I. in 1955. It was the next most important synthetic fibre to follow nylon (q.v.). (127)

Tights (129) (165) (166) (170)

Top hat (1) (18) (25) (49) (60)

Toque A small, turban-like hat without a brim; much favoured by Queen Mary. (95)

Trilby Soft felt hat with a brim and dented crown. Men's: (65) (69) (96) (144) (146). Women's: (123) (150)

Trousers (Women's). (36) (84) (86) (91) (112) (142) (145) (159) (160) (170). Trouser suits: (126) (129) (155) (169)

Tweed Woollen cloth in an open, plain or twill weave. (45) (82) (164)

Vionnet, Madeleine (43)

Voile A light, semi-transparent fabric. (15)

Waistcoat A close-fitting jacket without sleeves, usually buttoning at the centre front. Men's: (1) (119). Women's: (129) (152) (155)

War-time dress (36) (84) (87) (88) (91)

Watch-chain A long chain attached at one end to the watch, worn in the waistcoat pocket and fixed through a chain-hole in the front edge of the opposite side of the waistcoat. (10) (23) (144)

Wedding dress (12) (71)

Wedge shoe A shoe on which the sole and heel are formed in one in a wedge shape. Wedge shoes are often combined with platform soles (q.v.). (139) (160)

Winklepickers Slang term for the excessively narrow, pointed toes of shoes fashionable for men and women in the late 1950s, and early 1960s. It derives from the pins used to extract edible winkles from their shells. (121) (156)

Worth (54) (72) (97) (101)

Wrist watch (32) (61) (120) (149) (158) (167)